The
# COMPASS

Indie Publishing for the
Highly Motivated Author

By
Phil Whitmarsh

Dorodango Press
Lincoln, Nebraska

Summary: Focused information to help authors indie-publish their own books.
ISBN:
978-0-9903743-0-5 (online edition)
978-0-9903743-1-2 (printed edition)
978-0-9903743-2-9 (ePub edition)
978-0-9903743-3-6 (.mobi edition)
978-0-9903743-4-3 (audio book edition)

First Printed Edition – January 2015

Printed in the United States of America
by

*Redbrush*

1201 Infinity Court, Lincoln, Nebraska 68512
Toll-free: 855.379.6218

(#012015)

*For my father, Wayne.*
*Architect, activist, compass, dad.*

*He taught me the necessity of effort and*
*raised me to teach the wisdom of forethought.*
*Redbrush combines the two for the benefit of*
*writers, authors, and creators of all types.*

*Pass it on.*

The Compass

# Contents

The Compass

# Introduction

This guide has three specific goals. First, *The Compass* is put together to help you think of your book as the end product that you want it to be. *The Compass* will help you identify your targeted audiences, desired goals, and whatever successful destination you want to reach. Second, *The Compass* will—in plain, accessible language— cut through the hype and static to quickly and concisely guide you as you consider and choose the most appropriate publishing

**Why should I read this guide?**

The purpose of this book is to educate authors about their publishing options and confirm they have the vision, motivation, and ability to captain their publishing process. But, if you're the type of author who prefers to learn through direct contact, drop Redbrush an email (info@redbrush.com) or pick up the phone and give us a call at: 855-379-6218. We're happy to help!

process, based on your project and the goals you've identified. Finally, *The Compass* will introduce you to Redbrush. Redbrush is an indie-publishing services provider that wants to create long-term, successful relationships with highly motivated indie authors, artists, illustrators, and publishers.

I can't imagine a more satisfying way to spend a workday than helping creative and excited authors publish their writings and launch their books into the bookselling marketplace. Might you be one?

You may have noticed that the subtitle of this guide reads "for the highly motivated author." That's not a typographical error.

"Isn't every author motivated," you ask? Yes. I believe every writer hopes their work has value and relevance. But as soon as the last keystrokes of a manuscript have been struck, an author's excitement can begin to quickly fade as inevitable questions invade their thoughts.

"Is this any good?" "What do I do now?" "Who will ever read this, anyway?"

If your sole goal was just to write the manuscript and have the satisfaction of completing it, congratulations! Well done, you! You can close this guide now and bask in the satisfaction that you reached your goal of completing your manuscript. Done.

But if you've got that itch to do something more with your writing—what Wayne Dyer calls that "burning desire"—to impact others, make a difference, and share it with a world of readers, you need to know the path you'll follow to publish your book (and eBook ... and audiobook ... etc.). To follow that path, you'll need motivation. Some days, a lot of it.

If you have writing to share, you have more options than ever before. You can make choosing your path either simple or frustrating. You can hope to get an agent and have them represent you to traditional publishers. You can try a subsidy or vanity press publishing model, where you pay for costs of publishing with a publisher who will accept the rights to your book and earn most of the profits. Or—if you have the necessary motivation and confidence—you can do it yourself (DIY) and be your own publisher. There are advantages and disadvantages to each option.

Let's assume for now that you're considering the DIY option, to publish your book independently of traditional constraints and the vanity press publishing stigma.

Are you motivated enough to educate yourself and learn the ropes so that you can captain your publishing voyage? (Without a traditional or vanity press publisher calling the shots; this is self publishing, after all.) *The Compass* can provide the navigation and help you need to reach whatever destination you can identify. But if you're not motivated enough to learn how, take the wheel, and be the captain of your process, you're not the "highly motivated author" you need to be to successfully sail through to publication and on to successful seas.

"Why must I be the captain?"

No one will ever value your project more than you will. If you choose to work with Redbrush, you can be assured we'll take the greatest care to provide the best guidance and services, but if you aren't able to meet them at the wheel, your publishing project will founder like the Titanic.

Straight talk. That's one of the benefits of this guide—and working with Redbrush. *The Compass* is—and we are—focused on your project and process, not the hype. There are plenty of options out there with staff trained to cheer and flatter the credit card right out of your pocket on the first call. If cheerleading is more important than expert and timely direction, Redbrush might not be the best fit for you. How's that for straight talk? (Yes, we'll help you choose Redbrush or disqualify us—doing either with the greatest confidence.)

This guide will act as your compass—and a checklist of sorts— to help you expertly prepare for the publishing process you choose. Whether it's with Redbrush helping you indie-publish or not, the information here will help you turn your manuscript into one or many published products. I recommend you read *The Compass* from start to finish, then come back and jot questions or note areas where you might need intermediate direction. Once you've gotten through the guide, you'll be ready to speak about your goals, project, and process. Redbrush will be ready to listen.

This we will pledge: If you choose Redbrush to help you independently publish your creative works, we will partner with you to confidently publish the best products that you can. We will be motivated and committed partners to help you reach whatever goals for success you identify. That's right, we'll partner with you. Your success is our success.

You've made it through the introduction. Turn the page to start a quick but comprehensive view of the publishing process. We'll continue with practical, straight talk and insights, and leave the technical bits and bytes for the end of the guide.

Your next steps will determine the success of your book and your platform. I hope to see you on the next page. No matter what you decide, we wish the best success for you and your writing.

Thanks for considering Redbrush.

Phil Whitmarsh
Co-founder, Redbrush

# Where Do You Want To Go?

Most folks who arrive at Redbrush's website or doorstep want to start with questions about production costs. Sometimes that means they have press-ready files and are ready to print covers and interiors and have them bound as paperback or hardcover books. More often, they're imagining that the single most important and costly element of their project will be printing their book. They want to know what it will cost to get a hundred physical copies of their book, or a thousand, or ten. They may or may not be thinking of the intangible steps in the publishing process, like registering a copyright for their book, buying an ISBN (or ten), editing the manuscript, designing the files, or the cost of getting their printed books marketed and distributed.

Obviously, if you've never printed a book before, any printing price can sound like a lot or sound like a little—depending on so many variables unique to you and your particular project. And printing costs have little to do with a book's success. Let's look at the process a little differently. To start at the very beginning, let's consider the *destination*.

What do you want to accomplish by publishing your book or a digital eBook? What do you want to achieve? Think of it this way ...

Imagine that publishing is a lot like traveling. "Where do you want to go?" When talking with a travel agent—or using any one of many travel quoting sites online—the destination is the first variable to nail down.

Every day you're asked by several people what you want or where you want to go. At a restaurant, you read the menu and order what you'd like to eat. At the movie theater, you ask for a ticket to the movie you want to see. You tell the taxi driver where to take you. It's really not so different when it comes to your book and the publishing journey on which you want to embark.

Unfortunately, most authors don't know the questions to ask or what services they need. It's like walking into a pizza place and asking for a burger. The ingredients might be similar, but you're not going to get what you're looking for.

Would you believe there are some companies out there who are counting on the fact that you don't know what you don't know? Any time there's money at stake, you can bet there are going to be folks who will try a little sleight of hand to sell you something that won't meet your goals. But you won't know that yet, will you? Why?

Maybe you've not been asked or really haven't thought about your destination or goals for your book. Let's start here, keeping in mind that your goals will determine the kind of publishing process you'll experience and the budget you'll want to anticipate.

What do you want to accomplish?

Answers naturally run the gamut. Most writers have a very personal wish or set of goals for their project. Is this a "bucket list" kind of project—one to check off your life's to-do list? Will you be happy just to hold the book in your hand and give out a few copies to family and friends? Okay. There's nothing wrong with that.

Do you want to offer the book for sale on your own website? Do you want to sell books through online retailers, like Amazon, BN.com, and others? Would you like to see your book on library shelves? Do you hope to have the book accepted to be sold in local bookstores? Do you think your book would be successful if offered in other bookstores around the country and/or markets throughout the world?

Are you a public speaker or professional presenter who wants to sell books at the back of the room? Do you hold workshops and want to include your book in the event's materials?

Is yours a calling card kind of book, introducing you to business prospects? Are you a professional who wants to use your book to demonstrate your knowledge and experience as an expert to new customers?

Are you looking for mainstream success with mainstream audiences? Do you aspire to be a successful author in the literary world? Would you like a traditional publisher to eventually pick up your book and future projects? Would you like to quit your day job and devote more time to writing books?

If you can dream it, we can help you reach it—*if* we know what you want to do and where you want to go. Tell us! We'd love to hear! We need to know.

Before you can cast off on your dream voyage, there's a fair amount of preparation to complete. Get out those suitcases!

The Compass

# First Steps

Many authors are immediately concerned about protecting their creative works from theft, fraudulent use, or plagiarism. You may feel more at ease to know that anytime you take fingers to keyboard or pen to paper to create intellectual property, it's automatically owned by you. You own the copyright to your work. Your computer will time-stamp it. This is usually safe enough when you're in the process of writing and composing. If you are anticipating publishing your work, it's a good idea to register a formal copyright with the Library of Congress's Copyright Registration Office (www.copyright.gov).

You can register a formal copyright through the mail or electronically through the Copyright Registration Office's website. Once you've registered and received a receipt for your registration, it will take several months to receive the final registration notice and copyright number. The good news is that this number isn't necessary to move forward. While waiting for the formal registration information, you can continue on with your publishing preparations and process.

You may have heard of what is referred to as *the poor man's copyright*. This was accomplished by sending a printed copy of your manuscript or an archived copy on disk or drive to yourself via the US Postal Service. As long as the package was left unopened and stamped over the flap, this method provided a dated archive that would indicate that on a specific day, the material was in the possession of the inferred creator or author of the work. This method is no longer practical. If proof of ownership is important to you—or if you are concerned it might ever be—it's worth formally protecting your work and intellectual property with a formal copyright registration. A copyright on any initial version of your manuscript should be sufficient through to formal publication. You many choose to register a copyright on the final book too, but this is optional.

If you're planning to indie-publish your manuscript or intellectual property and sell it, you'll want to assign an ISBN (International Standard Book Number) to it. ISBNs are used internationally to identify the product and publisher in the commercial marketplace. Because the goal of publishing is to *make it public* to many audiences with different product preferences, it's necessary to have an ISBN assigned to each edition or version of your work.

If your project is a "bucket list" or "friends and family" book and you're anticipating never offering it for sale, it's not necessary to assign an ISBN. If you anticipate ever selling the product, or want to keep your options open, it's easy and inexpensive to purchase and assign an ISBN for your book. It's one of those ingredients that makes your book every bit as published as traditionally published books. The ISBN also identifies you as the book's publisher—an added element of control and ownership of your own work.

Copyright and ISBN registration can occur at just about any phase of your creative process. Once you're ready to commence with a publishing and printing process, it's a good idea to have your ISBN assigned and/or your copyright registered—or at least know when you'll take care of them.

Some authors wait to register the formal copyright on their published book, rather than their manuscript. By indicating the year of publication and using the copyright symbol (©) in your files and printed book, you're informing your readers of your claim of ownership. You can wait and register the formal copyright once your book is printed if you wish.

## How Many ISBNs?

ISBNs have a couple functions. The ISBN designates the publisher of the work and identifies a specific version of that work in the commercial marketplace. Because ISBNs are edition-specific, it's important to anticipate how many ISBNs you will need: one for each version/edition of your book product. You might need only one ISBN or as many as a half dozen per title.

Each printed edition needs its own ISBN. Here's how a traditional publisher would do it. If they start with a hardcover edition to launch a book, it will need an ISBN. If they bring out a paperback edition later, it will have its own ISBN, too. If they publish a revised edition and change more than 15 percent or so of the content or change the title to reflect the new edition, they need another ISBN.

eBook editions need their own ISBNs, too. There are several eBook versions you might offer. If you will offer your eBook for the Kindle (in .mobi format) it will need a specific ISBN. If you offer your eBook in ePub format, legible by the Nook, Kobo, and other popular readers, it will need another ISBN. Audio books and MP3 files each need their own ISBN.

Think of ISBNs like a model number. Because ISBNs are used to help identify different editions of a work, it also removes confusion when someone wants to track down a specific edition of your title. Most retailers require that the published works they sell have an ISBN.

Because ISBNs are international, each country designates an office or organization to administer them. (If you are not an American author/publisher, a quick Web search will help you locate the appropriate ISBN office in your country.) In the United States, R.R. Bowker is the ISBN administrator (www.myidentifiers.com). It's easy to purchase ISBNs from Bowker at their website (or from authorized channels).

Unless you anticipate needing only a single ISBN for one printed edition of the book, it's most cost-efficient to order a block of ISBNs, especially if you want to publish more than one title with several editions.

ISBN barcodes are another piece of the identifying puzzle. In addition to your ISBN, a barcode can be created to include your ISBN and your retail price—if you wish—on your book's back cover to make scanning possible at retail locations and libraries. If you're anticipating retail sales of any kind, it's a good idea to have the suggested retail price coded into what's called the EAN Bookland portion of the barcode. These are the five extra digits that appear to the right of the ISBN on the barcode. Some customers know how to read these codes. Most do not. Retail prices in US Dollars are prefixed with a "5." Prices noted in Canadian dollars are preceded by a "4." A barcode with "51295" in the EAN Bookland portion would reflect the book's retail price as $12.95 (USD).

## Why ISBNs Are So Important

While the ISBN identifies the edition of a published work, it also identifies a title's publisher. This can be a little confusing.

If your book were being published by Random House, they'd assign an ISBN that they own to your book, to identify the specific edition of the title and themselves as its publisher. Anyone looking up that ISBN through a bookstore or other source would see that Random House is the publisher of that title.

When you self-publish your own book, you own and assign the ISBNs to your title's editions. If you use a publishing services provider—like Redbrush—you still own and assign the ISBNs. If you choose a vanity press publisher—paying a company to be your title's publisher—they'll assign ISBNs that they own to your title's editions. These ISBNs will designate them as the publisher with the publishing rights to the book.

Why is this important? The publisher—the designated owner of the ISBN and holder of the publishing rights—gets to decide how to divide the revenues from sales of the book and related published products. In the case of the vanity press publishers, these companies usually assign the royalty amount paid to authors. Some of them allow author/clients to choose what royalties they are paid—as long as the publisher can determine the retail price of the book. Whether the author chooses the royalty amount or the vanity publisher designates the amount, it's important to know how that amount translates into dollars and cents. Often, royalties are based on the net of the net, after several expenses and costs are added to the formula. In the vanity press publishing model, the primary function is to maximize revenue from authors paying to add book products to the company's catalog. Any book sales that occur are gravy on top of revenues from authors.

When you work with Redbrush, you have the benefit of knowing in advance what the formula will be to determine exactly how much money you'll make from each sale from distribution partners. Redbrush authors earn 100 percent of the net profits from the direct sales they accomplish.

We want you to be your own indie publisher. We want you to hold the publishing rights to your title(s) and own the ISBNs that you assign to your commercial, published projects. This is what indie publishing is all about—being the captain of your own publishing process.

## Naming Your Publishing Entity

Because you will own your ISBN(s) and assign it/them to your work, you'll want to name your publishing entity—your publishing company. Call up your muse and put on your creative beanie!

When you buy books, you may or may not look to see who published them. If you look for the name on books you own, you'll probably find names of some familiar, traditional publishers: Random House, Simon & Schuster, and McGraw-Hill, to name just a couple. You typically don't see books published by John Smith Press or Jane Doe Publishing. "'Your Name Here' Publishing" is not a good idea.

Create a name that sounds like a small publishing company or independent publisher—because that's exactly what you are going to be: an indie publisher of products created for your ideal and targeted audiences.

## What's In a Name?

If you use social media, you've probably received plenty of name generators to discover your pirate name, your holiday elf name, and many more. Try something similar to create your publishing entity name. Add the name of the street where you first lived to your first pet's name, and see what you get ("Orchard & Beau Books"). Think of a favorite swimming lake or park from childhood and add it to your favorite vacation destination ("Conestoga Canyon Publishing").

You can create a name that relates to the subjects of your books or reinforces the genre in which you write—"Stone Financial" for your many books on investing, or "Tsunami Tears" for your saucy romance series. Don't choose a name that restricts you too much. If you want to publish books in several genres, you might choose a name that could be used for all of them, or simply create a new publisher name that fits better. It's totally up to you. You are your own indie publisher. Think "Indie."

Write down your top ten attempts and do Web searches to see if they've been used before by someone else. You might be able to create a variation on the name or choose words of similar meaning. You can also contact R.R. Bowker to see if a name has been used before. You can do preliminary research using just about any Web browser and at www.isbndb.com, too. You're a creative writer. Have fun with this!

Remember, the goal is to create a name for your publishing entity that doesn't scream, "Hey, I'm self-publishing this book!" While there's absolutely nothing wrong with independently publishing your own writing, some readers prefer traditionally published books.

Undeniably, there's been a stigma. "Vanity published, bad. Traditionally published, good!" Because there are so many options to get your book "out there"—with little care about editorial integrity or innovative design—there are a lot of books in the marketplace that haven't gone through any vetting or quality assurance process. There are a lot of vanity press publishers willing to publish anything a writer will pay to have published—no matter the editorial condition of the writing. It's no stretch to imagine how traditional publishers and the media and especially reviewers who report on and review published books feel about products from those companies and anyone who self-publishes without properly vetting their book for editorial integrity.

Our hope at Redbrush is that you're motivated to publish a superior product and help elevate the reputation of indie-published books, eBooks, and more.

## The Manuscript

Chances are you have or will soon have a final draft of your manuscript. Drafts are called "drafts" for a reason. They're clay. They're moldable. It's easy to tear off pieces and rework them or even pull them down and completely start over.

The initial function of your manuscript is to get your thoughts, ideas, story, and/or information down in written form. It's not supposed to be or expected to be perfect. It's not even expected to look like a book. Manuscripts look like ... well, manuscripts.

Keep it simple and create yours on a normal-sized sheet (8.5" x 11") with 1" margins all around. It's best to indent the first line of each paragraph. It's *not* necessary to hit the <SPACEBAR> twice after punctuation, nor is it necessary to tap the <RETURN> key twice at the end of a paragraph. (Your manuscript doesn't need extra lines between paragraphs.) Don't rely on too much bolded or underlined text. Let the words do the talking. Don't mess with formatting just yet. Keep it simple, scribe.

## When the Manuscript Is Done

There's a great sense of accomplishment just having completed the first draft of your manuscript. It's expected that you will have a sense of pride in your work. It's healthy to be a little skeptical, too. Remembering that most traditionally published books go through several editorial passes, try to humbly remember that the function of the first draft is to be a foundation for the book that follows. You should expect mistakes and errors throughout the work. Do what you can to find and correct them.

Even before you consider editorial services, you should go through your manuscript a couple different ways and times to be sure you've built the best manuscript you can. By the time you've completed your last draft, you've long since lost all objectivity with your book. Your brain probably knows it so well, you can speed read it with ease and your brain will actually read words that *are not there.*

One trick as you proofread is to shake up your manuscript's appearance. Most word processing programs will allow you to "select all" and change from one font to another easily. Change your original font to something else. If you've written your manuscript in a font with serifs like Times New Roman, switch it up to Arial or Helvetica. If you've been comfortable working in Arial, switch your entire manuscript over to Times New Roman or Garamond. Change the font size from 12 to 14 points, or from 12 to 10, or 10 to 12. This helps your brain read with refreshed objectivity. You'll find mistakes you've missed a hundred times before.

# Who, What, Where, When, and Why?

To keep your learning process interesting, let's alternate between instructional chapters and insightful information to help with bigger picture questions and issues.

## Who?

As you continue to think about your goals and desired destination ("Where Do You Want To Go?"), it's really important to know who your audience is. I often ask authors, "Who is your target audience; that group of what Stephen King refers to in his great book *On Writing* as your 'ideal reader'?"

You can always tell who's given their answer some thought and who hasn't:

"People who enjoy action and adventure stories with a real flair for technical detail. Fans of Tom Clancy's fiction will love my book."

"Folks wanting to try their hand at residential real estate investing."

"Anyone who can read at an 8th grade reading level."

"Fans of Agatha Christie's whodunit mysteries."

"If they're breathing, they'll love my book."

"Readers interested in giving urban fiction a chance, reading a story about a struggling preacher's son in South Chicago who turns to drug dealing to pay for his grandmother's care after she suffers a stroke."

The more clearly you can identify who will enjoy your book, the easier it is to reach out to them specifically.

Chances are you can identify several groups and audiences. Make a list or type an outline on your computer with each of these groups. For extra credit, start thinking about where each of these groups gets information about movies they like, music they listen to, and restaurants they choose. These communication paths will prove to be a vital part of your marketing plans for your book.

## What?

Think about how to describe your book in a couple of sentences, so you're ready anytime an "elevator pitch" is needed. An elevator pitch is your dynamic, thirty-second synopsis dropped into conversation, like on a short elevator ride.

"My book combines the seven principles of highly successful people with my own must-follow steps of high-end real estate sales."

"My novel takes the reader through what might be the last week of a death row inmate being readied for execution for a crime he didn't commit. If he admits to another, more terrible crime that he is guilty of, he might be able to delay his execution."

"This is a collection of poetry describing the life cycle of a person with developmental disabilities who overcame their challenges to write and publish their life story. This is my story!"

"My book shares how anyone with a few hours a week and $300 can easily build an automotive detailing business and add over $3,500 of part-time income over the next year."

## Where?

Does your book relate to a specific geographic area? Is your book about fly-fishing in the rivers of Montana? Does your book describe a kind of architecture specific to the southern United States? Is your children's book about an historical site, person, or event? Sometimes your book will relate specifically to people who live in that community. Other times it will appeal to anyone interested in a site, individual, or event. Sometimes your book will be the perfect product to sell to former members of a community, or tourists who frequent a place, or hosts who often welcome guests to their community (owners of bed and breakfasts). Who doesn't like to escape to a new place or different time? Books help readers travel throughout the world and universe in just a few pages.

## When?

Keep the schedule for your book in mind. Are there times of the year when it makes better sense to launch your title? Remembering that your book is always fresh and new to every new customer, carefully consider whether you'd like to have your book as quickly as possible or have it done correctly.

Is your project time-sensitive? Is it needed for a town celebrating its 150th birthday? Do you want to give copies to family at a reunion or holiday gathering? Is your book in response to changes in the economy or in the political landscape?

Try to remember that annual holidays come around every year, as do anniversaries and birthdays. If you've taken the time to write something that might appear to be time-sensitive, don't forget that it will be relevant *any time* a new reader discovers it. (It will *always* be loved and relevant to any family member or loved one.)

There may be a desire to rush the publishing process so as to meet what feels like an all-important deadline. Take a deep breath and remember that a good book is always relevant to the right, "ideal" reader.

Consider the "friends and family" project that you might think *must* be ready by a specific date. Ask yourself, "which is more important; to be 'on time,' or to make something I will be perfectly proud of—*not* embarrassed by—if they find the mistakes I missed because I skimmed my final proof too quickly?" Consider making that same mistake on a book you've prepared for the first of several conferences or workshops. It's better to take your time and be sure the product you produce is as great as it can be, rather than do damage control when you've rushed a book to market.

## Why?

This is a biggie; perhaps the biggest question you need to answer! Why did you write your book? What do you want to accomplish by publishing it and making it available in the bookselling marketplace? What motivates you?

Think carefully and specifically, as the answer(s) will help you decide most confidently on the path you want to take, the help you'll need, and the budget you'll anticipate.

I've heard from authors writing about their struggles with addiction and recovery that if they can help just one person, publishing their book will be worthwhile. I've worked with authors who want to simplify a complex problem and process so that others don't have to experience the same pitfalls that plague the system and result in unnecessary bureaucracy. Some authors have a magic number in mind. "I want to sell one hundred books." "I want to sell a thousand books." "I want to sell 100,000 books." What would feel like success to you?

"I want to break even." I hear that a lot, too. The fact is, the more work you do to identify who your audiences are, what you want to accomplish with your book, and how you'll outreach to those readers, the better chance you'll have of reaching your targeted readers and succeeding in selling books, eBooks, and more.

The more motivated you are, the more success you'll achieve. I wish I could say it was just that simple, but wishing doesn't make it so. More on that soon.

# Editing and Editorial Services

Editing is tricky stuff. Why is editing important?

*"Tuh-**mey**-toh." "Tuh-**mah**-toh." "Puh-**tey**-toh." Puh-**tah**-toh."*

"There." "They're." "Their."

"Two." "To." "Too." ... to note a few.

If you want to effectively communicate a thought or idea, information or claim, you have to be understood by your reader. The best way to be consistently understood is to write the way that most of your readers read. Book publishers use a style guide to make sure that all of the writings' fundamentals are consistent from book to book—grammar, punctuation, and writing standards. *The Chicago Manual of Style* is the most common style guide in the trade book publishing industry. If you want your book to read well and sell well, you'll want to adhere to the rules in *The Chicago Manual of Style*—CMS, for short.

Typing a manuscript in Word or some other word processing program—complete with spell check on—is a good start. To be sure you're publishing a book that meets common publishing standards, you'll want to reference *The Chicago Manual of Style*.

When is professional editing necessary? That depends on your goals for your title: When you want your book to meet the same professional standards of any traditionally published book in the marketplace. When you want your book to be the best reflection of you, your knowledge, and your platform. When you will be competing against books that were professionally edited before they were published. Whenever you'll compete against books from authors promoting and marketing more effectively than you are.

Whenever you want to offer readers the best product they can purchase from you with the confidence that, once they've read and loved your book, they'll share positive word of mouth about your book with others who may or may not also be in your targeted readership, but haven't yet heard about it.

"All of the above."

Another way to look at it is this: you've spent months—maybe even years—preparing, writing, rewriting, and proofing your own manuscript. How do you put a value on that creative process? How much was that time worth? How much are you willing to bet that you wrote your manuscript perfectly enough that your readers will not question your credibility if they find errors in your book?

For a "friends and family" kind of project, you may decide you don't want to have your manuscript professionally edited. (Your audience will love it despite any bumps and bruises.) You probably aren't going to buy and assign an ISBN either, nor will you be trying to build your professional or literary reputation with a book that's not been vetted by a professional editor and/or editing team.

Who will you get to edit your book? An editor colleague once suggested that a writer should never accept editorial assistance or feedback from anyone they gave birth to or wake up next to. I think that's pretty wise, but probably doesn't go far enough.

Consider this. Imagine that one of your friends—someone who knows of your writing aspirations—brings you *their* manuscript to read and wants your honest opinion of their work. You want to like it. You want it to be good. If it's great, you'll go out of your way to find something to improve. If it's horrible, you'll work just as hard to find some redeeming element to praise. But the fact is that you probably aren't any more qualified than they would be if you asked them to read and report on *your* writing. You are probably not a professional book editor. Neither are they. To put out the most professional product, you need more than friends and colleagues. You need professional help.

Friends generally like to help and offer ideas. They may feel like they're paying it forward or doing you a favor. The best favor they will ever do is recommending your published book to other friends and colleagues. Their positive word of mouth will be priceless. Should they also help you with professional editing? Nope. There's too much in the balance.

The well-meaning school Language Arts teacher might seem like a good choice, as would a college English professor, but unless they moonlight as professional book editors, they're probably not. Because book editing is a profession and discipline unto itself—and very specialized—having someone who edits for a living is one of the best investments you can make in your book. The goal of a professional book editor is to help you publish the best book you can write. Nothing is more important to them than that.

When I'm asked for a professional, editorial opinion, I remind myself that I don't always know if a fine art painting is good or not, but I know if I like it or if it resonates with me. You wouldn't want me critiquing anything from Picasso's blue period. If you want professional criticism, you have to go to a professional critic. For professional-level editing, go to a professional. Doesn't your book deserve it?

## What Type of Editing?

Imagine that a big traditional publisher was going to publish your book. They would have several professional editors read your book, each one providing a specific type of editing during their own individual pass.

When you indie-publish your own book, you get to decide your title's level of editorial integrity. Because you are the publisher, you decide if it's going to read well and be pleasing to your readers, or not. It's no different than if you were offering your garage band's recorded, original music on iTunes. You can decide if it sounds amazing or … not so much. It's the same with your book.

There are three levels of editing that are offered at Redbrush: Level 1 Mechanical Editing, Level 2 Substantive Editing, and Level 3 Developmental Editing. We can also customize just about any editing service you need. Proofreading, ghost writing, indexing, and translating services are also available.

Think of a Mechanical Edit as an editing process to correct spelling, grammar, and punctuation—the basic mechanical building blocks of your manuscript. A Substantive Edit is a more substantial pass where issues like tense, syntax, and sentence structure are also addressed. Finally, for books that need help at a deeper, structural depth—help with the overall structure and effectiveness of the material—we offer a Developmental Edit. Each subsequent level is more complex and costly than the previous one—and requires more time to complete.

Each editing level is priced on a per word basis. Why not charge an hourly rate, like some online freelancers? We believe charging on a per word basis is the most consistent and fairest way to charge for the attention given to each and every word of your manuscript. While it might sound attractive when a freelancer suggests an estimated number of hours, it's common to get a low-balled quote that has to be adjusted once or twice during the subsequent editing process. It's difficult to change course mid-stream, when you feel your project's held hostage and the cost keeps going up and up … and they know it.

Redbrush can help you decide which level of editing is appropriate for your project. Whether you've had no professional feedback or already had your book gone through by someone/anyone—and need to confirm that your manuscript is ready for the next step—consider Redbrush's Editorial Appraisal Services. An editor will be assigned to evaluate the manuscript and confirm what—if any—editing would improve the integrity of your manuscript.

After you've done all you can confidently do yourself—that is the perfect time to have your book's editorial integrity appraised. Redbrush also offers a Book Marketing Appraisal to have your manuscript's marketing potential and viability reviewed. This can also help you determine if editing will increase your book's ability to meet your identified goals.

Remember, your book's editorial integrity and how effectively it communicates your ideas, message, or story will leave the lasting impression with your reader. Neither a flashy cover nor catchy title will impact your reader more than how well your book reads. Keep that in mind as you consider the editing segment of your publishing journey.

The Compass

# Challenges, Choices, and Squalls

This guide wouldn't be complete without some cautions and reminders about the realities of the publishing industry.

Chances are you wouldn't be considering a DIY (Do-It-Yourself) indie publishing model if you had an agent and/or traditional publisher beating down your door. The landscape has changed a lot over the last few years. The publishing industry has seen a lot of change and evolution.

## The Traditional Path

While you have more options than ever to get your writing published, traditional publishing remains the most unlikely. In the traditional publishing model, a writer seeks out agency representation, hoping someone will feel the love for *and* recognize the great commercial potential of their manuscript. Once an agent sees the value and shares the vision, that agent solicits traditional publishers with hopes to sell the rights to the book so that a publisher will publish it. Everyone makes money on the success. The risk resides with the publisher. The competition for publisher attention is fierce.

Traditional publishing has been and remains very expensive for the publisher. Once a title's been acquired, publishers invest in several editorial passes to properly prepare the manuscript. Marketing teams work with focus groups to determine the best title, cover, and presentation for the book. Designers then layout and design those pleasing cover and interior files from which to print.

Where typesetters used to layout the lead type to build the pages and signatures to be sent to the presses, now typesetting is done on computers. Printers then print the books. A publisher's sales teams would have already been in the field for months, promoting it among the next season's titles to distributors and retail buyers.

The challenge has always been that there are many hopeful writers out there and a finite number of agents, publishers, and opportunities to promote book products in this traditional model. Because bookstores can't possibly stock all of a year's new titles *and* last year's successes *and* "the classics," publishers have limited the number of titles they launch in a given season and year.

Don't imagine that because someone gets a publishing deal their book's launch is a sure thing. Executive management is so fluid at traditional houses, any personnel changes can result in a coordinating editor's already-approved projects being scrapped. Books that showed enough promise for deals and might only be months from release can be sent back to the slush pile on a whim. It happens all the time.

Thanks to Internet sales and electronic editions of books, competing for shelf space isn't as important as it used to be. With eBook sales growing so quickly, some have argued that shelf space has become practically irrelevant.

While the opportunity to self-publish makes it possible for just about anyone to publish just about anything, it also makes the challenge of reaching your targeted readers all the more important. Though traditional publishers still publish a few thousand titles each year (total), vanity press publishers and independent publishing authors (like you) add *several hundred thousand* new titles to the available products in the marketplace.

If you think of the traditional publishing industry and process as the gatekeepers of the sacred publishing possibilities, the increase in publishing opportunities has taken down many of the barriers that kept most writers from ever seeing their work in book form. Now there are lots of options.

This proliferation of possibilities, materials, and products makes it all the more important to fine-tune your product to make your book as viable as it can be. The better your book, the greater your chance of successfully achieving your identified goals. How you prepare your material, build your book, and promote it in the marketplace will make the difference in how successful you and your book(s) will be.

Digital, computer-based layout and design have streamlined the production process. Conventional lead type typesetting has gone the way of the dodo. Traditional publishing processes can still take eighteen to twenty-four months, as publishers move their precious, chosen few through the many steps to publication, launch, and promotion.

Redbrush has abbreviated the traditional time frame. Depending on the services that you need, you can hold your book in your hands in as little as a few weeks. Even starting with the last draft of your manuscript, or starting with ghostwriting assistance, you can anticipate a journey of a few months, not years. It's never a good idea to rush the process. A manuscript naturally needs time to evolve—or gestate—to be fully readied for publication. If yours is a frantic process, chances are something will get missed or mistakes will be introduced. Anytime humans are involved in the creative process, mistakes can occur. Book publishing is one of the most detail-oriented processes ever created. Anticipating a more detail-oriented and methodical process will help you catch errors and correct them. The end results will be all the sweeter if you take full advantage of the time and intentional process to come.

## Vanity Press Publishing

Vanity press publishing is paying to be published. It's *big* business. If you choose to work with a vanity press publisher, you'll sign a contract or publishing agreement that *gives* them the publishing rights to your book, so they can publish and print it. Though you will, in most cases, still own the rights to your book, you're basically granting them a free license to be its publisher for as long as you choose to work with them. You will accept or, in some cases, choose a royalty amount that you will be paid if your book sells. All risk resides with you.

In the vanity press publishing model, an author usually purchases a publishing package that includes some of the services and steps that your book must complete to be published, printed, and made available in the marketplace. ISBNs owned by the vanity press publisher—NOT you—are assigned/given/included with the package. They designate the vanity press company as the publisher of the work. The press-ready files that are necessary and designed to print your book are retained by the vanity press publisher. They own these files and they are copyright protected. This can be confusing. Your book's manuscript is yours. You own the intellectual property, but the publisher owns the files created to publish and print your books. (Sure, you can have them for a fee. See: Ransom.) Even if you provide almost-ready files, they'll still need to make adjustments to add the ISBN, barcode, and other information on the copyright page, and save final PDF versions of the files. The vanity press publisher owns and controls them.

One of the challenges of working with any vanity press publisher is that you've basically given away your publishing rights and thus control of your project. While you may have input about the cover, layout and design, and other elements related to your title, the vanity publisher may have final say. *They* are the publisher, after all. (Check out the publishing agreement or contract that you are required to sign when you start your project to see just how much control you do or don't have.) Your ability to veto may only be in the right to cancel the process entirely, often forfeiting the majority of your funds/costs to date, if not all of them. While you may have some input, the vanity press publisher will decide the retail price for your book. Or, if they let you choose the retail price, expect it to affect your royalty.

Often, their publishing packages include a few "free" copies of your book, solely as a carrot, an enticement. In the case of many vanity press-published titles, these will be the only copies of the book that are ever printed.

Once your book is underway, the vanity press publishing company typically reminds you "what good is a published book, if you're not promoting it?" They're happy to sell a wide range of marketing and promotional services to help you advertise your book and better compete against traditionally published books— and all of their other clients.

With any vanity press publishing model and company, you get what you pay for. Buyers beware. The primary goal of most vanity press publishers is to gain revenue from their authors and get their published product "out there," one that may or may not sell any copies ever. The more publishing packages they offer, the more expensive they are, and the louder they cheer.

You can't buy success. If you buy package A, you'll receive the services included with that package. The gold package might get you another set of services, maybe more books, nothing more. The diamond package includes its set of services and support. That's it. No package includes or can guarantee success. You can only pre-pare and hope for it. Their trained cheerleaders can sure make any advanced package seem reasonable for your extraordinary book.

What do you get for the cost of that gold, purple, or ruby package? You have your book in your hand. The package probably included file design, a few corrections, a few copies, and possibly having it available through popular online bookselling websites, maybe not. But when your book is published, that's *all* it is ... published. It has only a slightly greater chance of success than your manuscript. It hopefully looks nicer.

This is one of the drawbacks of these anyone-can-publish-any-thing days: the dilution of "published" status as the Litmus test for better quality.

"Will it sell?" While that is the most important question you should ask about your title early in the process, it's probably the most irrelevant question you can ask if you've published through a vanity press publisher.

Vanity press publishers make their money—a lot of money—selling publishing services to their authors. Paid publishing packages result in new books in their company catalogs. If the title doesn't sell, that's okay. Its publishing process was paid for by the author. No risk. Nothing lost. If the book sells, great. The publisher benefits from the gravy and shares a small portion of it with the author in the form of a royalty. No risk there.

Remember, vanity press publishing is big business. One large vanity press company has been busy buying up smaller ones over the last few years, to gobble up as many segments of the self-publishing market as they can. They operate as a large consortium of vanity press brands, each targeting a specific kind of author or segment of the marketplace. Would you be surprised to know that these companies can only boast that their titles sell an average of less than one hundred copies each—during the lifetime of the book? Their CEO proudly reported this to the *New York Times* ... twice.

Have you identified the number of books you'd like to sell? Was that number more or less than one hundred copies?

There's a relevant quote I'd like to share here. "Characterize people by their actions, and you'll never be fooled by their words." (That guru Anonymous said some amazing things!) Knowing that much of the vanity press industry counts on you not knowing what you don't know, it's never been more important to clearly determine what you want to accomplish and who can help you reach your goals.

Your publishing goals should include control over your project, ownership of the title's ISBN(s), ownership of your printing files, and the publisher's profits for the sale of your book.

That brings us to ...

## Redbrush Indie Publishing

What if you could experience the same comprehensive publishing process that a traditional publisher goes through and end up with a chance to build greater success with your title, platform, and brand than you can if you choose a vanity press option?

Redbrush offers the same professional quality and opportunities to reach your identified goals that you would expect from a traditional publisher. It's one of a few companies that offers you the opportunity to own your ISBNs, control your publishing rights, be your own publisher, and profit from the investment you make in your book and your platform. Unlike any other company in the industry, Redbrush helps you prepare for and build better success with your book, platform, and brand. How do we do this?

As in the vanity press publishing model, you'll pay for the services and support you need to publish your book and launch it into the bookselling marketplace. But *unlike* the vanity press path, we help *you* clearly decide what success you want to achieve and determine whether or not your book can make that happen—and receive expert guidance at every step. *You* will determine the success you want to achieve and decide to publish a book that can reach those goals. *You* will be the publisher. *You* will own your files. *You* will earn the publisher's profits from your book sales. That is the difference, in a nutshell. How is that for incentive? Sounds pretty great, doesn't it? It's like beating the traditional publishers at their own game, while turning away from a vanity press publishing option that provides little or no meaningful return for the author's investment.

One of the loudest complaints about the vanity press publishing model is that authors pay for the publishing of their book, but they don't earn the publisher's profits. The author takes all the risk, but doesn't receive the greatest rewards. (Why so many authors are not aware of this from the start is curious. "Motivated" authors whose projects are intentional should never fall into this tiger trap.)

With Redbrush, you can receive expert guidance, professional publishing services, quality book products, dynamic Web presence, effective marketing support, and have the greatest chance of reaching the success you desire by partnering with a specialized, seasoned team—all at fair and competitive prices.

You get to decide if your book is a sparkler to delight a single, special child, a bonfire to brighten your community of friends and loved ones, or a wildfire set to enlighten the whole world. Whether your goal is to simply hold a single copy of your published book in your hands or take the market by storm, putting thousands of copies into the hands of your ideal readers, Redbrush can help you reach your destination.

# Design Services

Book editors edit. Book designers layout and design book files. Some people are confused about these steps, imagining that the designer completes the editing while laying out the book. This is neither possible nor practical.

Just as editing is a professional discipline requiring training, practice, and experience, book design requires a lot of education and practice to adhere to the publishing conventions and standards common in the book publishing industry. They create print-ready PDF cover and interior files that are moved to the book printing department to print copies of your bouncing baby book!

As with most products, books are designed and printed in standard sizes. The most common trade paperback sizes for black and white books are 6"x9", 5.5"x8.5", and 5"x8". You can also go a little larger if you like: 7"x10" or 8.25"x11". Full-color books also have common sizes, depending on the orientation of layout and design. Standard sizes for full-color books are 8"x8", 8"x10", 10"x8", and 8.5"x11". (Remember, when talking about your book's trim size, the first dimension given is for the width of the book and the second is the height.)

These standard sizes can most easily be printed cost-efficiently. Printing something outside of the most common sizes is certainly possible, but can cost more as adjustments need to be made to accommodate the variance from standard sizes.

You've seen books of other sizes, like mass market paperbacks printed on very inexpensive newsprint and sold everywhere from grocery checkout lanes to drugstores. They're cost-efficient if you're printing tens of thousands of copies. You've probably seen oversized coffee table books. It's difficult to make anything outside of the norm cost-efficient without printing thousands of copies to bring the per unit price down. Printing within the standard trade sizes is the most cost-efficient way to go for an indie book publisher like you.

My father was an architect, so it's in my blood to enjoy seeing a book take shape on the screen, whether a designer takes a napkin sketch or notes from an author consultation to build the files for the printed book, or conjures them from a blank screen. When authors ask "how much will my book cost?" or "how much is design?" I'm reminded of standing on a vacant lot with my dad—who occasionally freelanced for people wanting to build a one-of-a-kind residence—his excited client, and a building contractor. The client asked, "How much will it cost?"

Pop would ask back, "How many square feet do you want? How many bedrooms? Bathrooms? Will there be a breakfast nook and a formal dining room? Family room and formal living room? Swimming pool? Finished basement?"

The contractor would chime in. "Wood floors or marble? Nine foot ceilings or twelve? Standard or custom windows? One stall garage ... or three?" And on and on.

Having a clear vision of your book and end product(s) in mind as you start the publishing process is helpful. Being able to describe your cover ideas and whether the interior of the book needs any-thing special will be vitally important to the book designer. What do you want to communicate with your cover? What do you want the reader/customer to feel when they see it? This isn't as difficult as it seems. Here's an easy way to start.

## Bookstore Field Trip

Plan a field trip to your local bookstore. Chances are you have a large retailer or a small, independent bookstore nearby. Here are some easy exercises to start thinking about how your book should be designed and built.

Walk to the shelf where the bestsellers are placed with their covers facing out. Squint from a few feet back and note what colors you see. What colors are used most? What colors stand out from the background best? What shapes and layouts draw you in?

Open your eyes a bit more and read the titles. What fonts—the style of the letters—are easiest to read? Which do you like? What text colors catch your eye?

Now look at the imagery or illustration on the covers. How do they complement the colors and fonts? You may see nonfiction books featuring their author on the cover in a very professional and attractive portrait. Some book covers have an illustration, photo, or collage as the focal point. Sometimes the image is literal—a line of motorcycles on the cover of a book about ... yep, motorcycles. Sometimes the image is more abstract to communicate a feeling or mood, or invoke a response. You might see a dove flying in front of rays of light on a spiritual book about recovery or grief. Would a close-up image of several people's hands communicate community? Harmony? Would two facing lines of raise hands and fists communicate adversity? Conflict?

One primary function of the front cover is to draw you in, to get you to pause and turn the book over to read the information on the back. Considering the whole cover, what would make you pick up a book and read the back cover information? Is there anything about one book that grabs your attention more than the next? Is there anything tugging your emotional attention?

Now, go to the section of the store that most closely matches where your title would be. Look at books that might be similar to yours. (Sometimes the books that help most will be in a totally different area or genre. Don't be afraid to browse other sections.) Compare and contrast these books. See what they have in common. Which cause you to think "professional" or "credible"? Are there any covers that you don't like? Why? Sometimes, knowing what turns your customer off is as important as knowing what turns them on.

The front cover is intended to give readers (read: customers) a positive first impression. The back cover provides an important second impression. Because people do judge books by their covers—and everything on them—it's important for your cover to look as professional as possible.

Turn books over to get a feel for what they're about. Some books will have a back-of-the-book description. Some will have blurbs and excerpts from reviews of the book or a previous title. If the cover gives the first impression, it's the back cover that gives the second impression. It's often the back of the book that confirms for the reader that they've found the right product and seals the deal. Likewise, covers and back covers can just as easily disqualify a book. As you think about your book's layout and design, imagine what your ideal reader and customer would need to see and read to confidently choose it. If you are a member of your ideal audience, imagine what would get you to buy your own book. Chances are, what attracts you will attract readers like you to your title. What would make you say, "Aha! This is exactly what I'm looking for"?

When guiding authors to think about their title and cover, I often suggest that they make sure their book's cover has the "huh?" factor. Selling is about capturing a customer's attention and prodding their imagination. "What could this title mean?" "How does the cover image relate to the title and the story within?" Anything that gives a customer a moment's pause gives you a better chance of causing them to investigate further and of closing the sale. The photos mentioned above (symbolizing relationships between groups of people) will hopefully make customers take a moment to see how the images reinforce the title or theme of the book.

I hope the name "Redbrush" generated a "huh?" moment for you. Perhaps you asked, "What is a Redbrush?" Perhaps that curiosity caused you to pause long enough to realize something extraordinary is located at www.redbrush.com. It's got to be the same with your book. Let's draw people to it! Which of the following covers would make you curious about a book?

- A novel, *Some Happy Marriage*, with a cover image of a smoking chainsaw next to the freshly sawn half of a loveseat, stuffing still floating in the air.

- A nonfiction biography called *The Red Tractor* with a cover shot of a *green* antique John Deere farm tractor.

- An anthology of poetry by a high school senior class, with an old class photo of first graders, and the title, *Not All Survived*. Wouldn't that make you wonder which of these cute kids didn't make it to high school graduation?

We're here to help you imagine your book and cover and the success they can bring. What will make your dream a reality?

## Cover Design

Whether yours is a book of poetry, a novel, nonfiction, or the next big thing in the self-help genre, you need to make a good first impression. Maybe the field trip's given you some ideas.

Cover design and all of our design services are priced based on the time and amount of creativity it takes to create and complete your cover. As the captain and publisher of your book, you will decide what is presented to your audiences. Redbrush offers you the control over your design process. You can choose for us to build something from scratch or start with some patterned examples to follow.

If yours is a bucket list or "friends and family" kind of project, Redbrush offers several cover patterns from which to start. You may not have high expectations, but want something that looks professional and won't turn people away. You can provide the text you want to appear on the front cover, spine, and back cover; a photo or illustration for the front cover and an author's photo for the back cover, if you like. Let us know if you have a color scheme in mind, and we'll build this cover for you quickly and less expensively.

Custom design requires more creativity and time, so it will cost more. The designer you work with can provide a couple mocked-up samples to make sure we're on the right track. If you require special graphical editing in Photoshop, collaging of images, or anything that adds more time than what's included, you can expect to pay a little more.

The more deluxe your cover, the more time and creativity will be required to build something completely from scratch, and give you several mock-ups from which to start. It's a little like our designer's pitching ideas and concepts to you as if you were an advertising client. The more time and work you need to custom build your book's cover, the more costly the Deluxe Cover Design service will be.

If your book is a hardcover book with a dust jacket, you'll need to have another cover file created to be printed and folded around the book's shell. This costs a little more, too.

## Interior Design

Book interiors require a very different kind of design process. Covers are usually built in a graphical design program like Adobe Photoshop or Illustrator. Multi-page interior files are best created in Adobe InDesign or QuarkXPress. These are expensive, professional design programs with quite a learning curve. Our designers have trained and used these programs for years. It isn't practical for authors to purchase and learn these programs. Our teams are fast, responsive, professional, and know how to build what you're seeking.

Using the home building example again, a building contractor might subcontract out the laying of a house's foundation to let specialists do it faster and better. They don't have a roofing team put up your house's walls, and so on.

For novels, memoirs, and even some nonfiction works presented in paragraph, prose form, we offer a selection of patterned layouts with specific styles to be applied to complete interior designs. You can choose from some fairly common appearances and patterns and have a professional book that looks like it came from a traditional publisher.

The patterns are set up to fit publishing standards with the right font size, leading, margins, and so on. It's important to have your book fit the standards that readers are used to and expecting in the books they purchase. Why is this so important? If a book's body text is a particular size, it has a corresponding leading or line height that looks the best and allows for faster reading and retention of the information or story. If the line height is too tight (short), the text is more difficult to read and downright unpleasant to read for long periods of time. This is just one of the factors that helps readers enjoy a book longer and without tiring, looking for interruptions, or other excuses to put a book down. The longer they can comfortably read, the more they'll enjoy the book. The more they like the book, the more likely they'll be to recommend it to others.

If your book has graphics, illustrations, photos, tables, bulleted lists, or any other non-text elements, it will require more time and creativity on the part of the designer to complete your book's final interior appearance. The more elements that require individual formatting or design help, the longer it will take to complete the design, and the more costly it will be.

Deluxe design—for very complex works like textbooks or graphic-intensive "coffee table books"—is priced based on the number of formatting elements required in the book. Again, time and the number of non-text elements will contribute to the cost of interior design.

## Children's Books, eBooks, and Other Design Needs

There are design and publishing standards to be followed. The designs of children's books and other specialty projects are priced based on the anticipated time to take the illustrations that you have provided or had us create and create the files necessary to print copies of the book. Most children's books are either 24 or 32 pages. If your book is longer, you will spend a little more for the additional time to complete your files.

eBook, Web design, and other specialized work is priced fairly to be competitive in the marketplace and help your support materials have a comprehensive and consistent appearance. We want your book, platform, and brand to look great and for all of their elements to complement each other well.

## DIY Design

While it may be possible to use a program that you have to build your own rudimentary files for book printing, we recommend you have a professional book design team build the files you need and convert them to PDF so that they can be printed or converted to eBook programs for eBook editions. PDF conversion provides another opportunity for files to corrupt and for errors to be introduced. This requires a very close eye when files are proofed.

Again, you probably aren't aware of the publishing standards that look best in a book of fiction or what's most appropriate in a nonfiction work. Your book's interior and its readability will directly affect the reader's enjoyment and satisfaction with it. If it causes any discomfort—usually such an unconscious effect that readers are not even aware of it—they are more likely to put it down sooner. Remember, the cover makes the first impression, followed by the back cover text's second impression. It's the lasting impression provided by the layout and design as well as the information in the book itself that will determine its success in the marketplace ... or its failure. We don't recommend you risk your book's success on the slim chance that you might be able to create a design that looks pretty good. "Pretty good" isn't good enough.

Every print job that we do includes a Pre-Flight check of the title's files to make sure they comply with the Printing File Requirements. If the files you provide don't comply, you'll have the choice of fixing them yourself, or having our Pre-Flight team correct the files for a fee. As we go to press, their rate is $90 per hour, with a half hour minimum.

# Bringing It All Together

Once your writing is done, you're comfortable with the editorial quality and integrity of your manuscript, and you have completed files to print, it's time to print books!

Because this is your book, you'll want and be expected to proof each step. You'll read through the edited files. You'll go through the designed files. After proofing and any corrections have been made, you will be confident that it's time to birth this book!

By the time the files are ready, you'll have a good idea how many books you want to print to get started. Your identified goals will help you determine how many copies to print. Hopefully, you've been thinking about this stage as part of a greater process, so you have an idea of where to start with printing quotes.

If yours is a "friends and family" book, you might simply need to count up the number of family members and loved ones that you want to give copies to and print that number or as close to it as you can. If your book shares family history or is your personal memoir, be sure to anticipate extra copies that will be given to the family's children as they get older.

If you want to test the market and try to get some reviews and endorsements to see how the book is received, you have the option of printing Advance Review Copies (ARCs; sometimes called Advance Reader Copies and Advance Review Editions—AREs). ARCs usually feature artwork that is the same as or similar to the final printed books and are labeled as an "Uncorrected Advance Review Copy" to let people know that it may not have been through its last proofreading stage. Sometimes the words "Not For Sale" are included.

Traditional publishers often print and distribute ARCs to their sales teams, retail buyers, and reviewers who they hope will write endorsements or blurbs to be used in marketing materials. While big, traditional publishers might print several hundred ARC copies, you will probably need no more than fifty to one hundred.

ARCs can sometimes become collectible should you and your book achieve literary or critical success in the future.

Another way to test the market is to print a smaller print run of books to share with your friends, family, colleagues, boosters, and few media contacts, to see how the book is received. This test printing is a great way to see how readers who are not your family and loved ones like the book and determine how big to go with your subsequent press runs. (It's also a good chance to catch previously missed typos.)

## Booster Copies and an ARC Exercise

Try this exercise. Take out a piece of paper or open a page in your word processing program and list your boosters. List every person who's ever said, "Gosh, just let me know when your book's printed. I'll be first in line to buy a copy!" or something like that. There is no better feeling than getting to tell those loved ones and colleagues that it's time to put their money where their mouth is!

Add to your list any family members, other friends, high school chums, and business contacts that you're sure you'll either sell or give a copy to. Don't forget the friends from the water cooler, the manager at the bookstore you've pestered with questions, your friends who read and share new authors and books with you from time to time, and the Facebook friends who've been providing *attaboys* and *waytogos* through the last several months (or years). Add the names of your media contacts—the folks who work at the radio station, the friend of the friend who works at the newspaper, and that pal who blogs about the subject about which you're writing.

Add all of those names up. The resulting list will probably have between fifty to one hundred names. Anticipate that each of the people on your list might have a friend or colleague they want to share a copy with, and consider *doubling* the previous total. If you're going to test the water first, be ready to print a first press run of either one hundred books or a number twice as big as your "booster list"—whichever is greater.

Can't you just feel the labor pains? The book stork is on the runway!

The Compass

# Printing Books

There is something magical about its arrival. After what feels like endless months of waiting, it's here. You can hold it in your hands and feel great that everything's turned out okay. The arrival of a child or grandchild is something magical to behold. Your book's arrival might just be the most moving experience in your creative life.

I've received calls and emails from overwhelmed authors when their books arrived. Opening those cartons and seeing their book for the first time has been exhilarating, humbling, spiritual, and terrifying. Expect a lot of emotions! The months or years of writing and dreaming have arrived in a neat, printed, bound package. Sorry, but the arrival of an eBook will never be as exciting as your printed book's birth. Nothing makes it all as real or as worthwhile as receiving physical, printed copies of your book. Celebrate and savor these milestone moments!

## What Goes In

To print books, you need print-ready PDF files. If you're printing paperback books, you need a cover PDF file and an interior PDF that's in single-page layout. If you're doing a casewrap hardcover book, where the printed cover is adhered to the hardcover's shell and laminated, you'll still need just two PDF files. If you're doing a hardcover book with a casewrap and a dust jacket, or a cloth-bound hardcover book with a dust jacket, you'll need a third press-ready file for the dust jacket—in addition to the casewrap cover or title-stamped file for the cloth-bound cover.

With the evolution in book printing, you can print almost anything you can imagine. But the fact remains, what goes in is what comes out. In the lead typesetting days, a nicked lead letter would result in a nicked letter on every page the plate printed. The same is true of digital files. If there is a mistake in the PDF files from which the books are printed, that mistake will be in every copy of your book. This is why it's so important to be sure your press-ready files are ready to go and as correct as you can make them.

Remember, publishing is a human endeavor, and even the best traditionally published books have errors. There's practically no such thing as a perfect book. The great news is that because you hold the reins of your book, you can choose to fix a mistake in the next printing. Easy. Expect a great product, not a perfect product, and you'll be fine and your blood pressure will be, too.

## Printing Stocks

Your files will be set up to print the components of your book: the cover, a dust jacket—if appropriate—and the interior book block. If yours is a black and white interior book (b/w), a novel for example, it will be printed on a one-ink press. The cover will be printed on a four-color ("full-color") printing press. You will choose the cover and interior stock that makes the best sense for your book's type based on the design and elements within it.

Interior paper stocks are very important and should also be selected based on the type of book you're printing and publishing.

## Fiction

The average trade book is usually about 256 pages. Some novels are much longer. Novellas are shorter. One goal of any fiction writer is for their reader to enjoy the book well enough to read for long periods of time. The more one enjoys a book, the longer they'll read. The longer they read, the greater their satisfaction with the book—we hope! The greater their satisfaction with the book, the more friends and colleagues they'll likely tell about the book. Off-white paper stocks help them do this.

If a novel is printed on white paper, the contrast between the page and the text is at its greatest. The severity of this contrast can tire a reader's eyes more quickly, possibly causing them to put down an otherwise terrific book. To help the reader read more comfortably for as long as they choose to, fiction books are often printed on an off-white paper stock. It's often called "natural" or "cream." This off-white stock lowers the contrast and doesn't tire eyes as quickly. Your readers can read much longer, enjoy greater satisfaction with the book, and be more likely to share information with others about it. Everybody wins.

Nonfiction memoirs written in prose style form might also be more suitable for off-white paper stocks. Photographs or illustrations that might be present in memoirs or even some fiction books still look great on these papers. If the author's desire is that the reader read for longer time periods, consider the off-white stock options. These are commonly offered in 50# and 60# weights, 50# being adequate and less expensive.

## Nonfiction

People tend to read nonfiction books a little differently than novels. Depending on the subject matter and reader's time, nonfiction books can either be read for long or short periods of time. Because nonfiction books are usually broken up by chapters with sections or sub-sections of information, it's easier to read for shorter periods of time, take breaks, and come back to pick up where you left off.

Nonfiction often has a different, more sophisticated presentation. Nonfiction customers will pay more to be informed than to be entertained. Bright white paper and the resulting high contrast that's challenging for fiction is ideal for nonfiction books. The brightness of the paper says "prestige" and "professional" to the reader. White interior paper stocks are available in several weights, the 50# and 60# paper weights being the most common. They're also the most cost-efficient choices as they are industry standard.

A stock's weight is an interesting thing. The paper weight is determined by weighing five hundred sheets of that particular stock. The large printing sheets that are used by some book printing presses are 25"x38". If you take five hundred sheets of the 60# stock, the stack should weigh sixty pounds. Five hundred sheets of the 50# stock will weigh ... yep, fifty pounds. The weight of the paper can affect the opacity of the pages—how much light and printed elements on the other side will show through. This really isn't the effect of ink actually bleeding through the paper, but a shadow effect caused by the paper's natural translucence.

50# stock is ideal for books with no or few images or illustrations. 60# stock is better if there are several or lots of images or illustrations. The 60# stock is more opaque with less shadow effect coming through the pages.

It's important to pick the right paper stock for your book project. There are standard paper stocks from which to choose. You wouldn't want to print your hardcover book on the same stock you run through your photocopier. Heavy wood-pulp based stocks, like the newsprint used for smaller, mass market books you find at the airport and drugstores should never be used for your trade paperback or hardcover books. Paper is one of the material costs of book printing and accounts for about half of your print job's expense. Check out published books you own or at the library and bookstore to see what you like and what's appropriate for your book.

## Quantity

Let your goals define your quantity and let the quantity define the best printing method or "platform."

A traditional publisher wouldn't print fewer than a few thousand copies to launch a book. A vanity press publisher prints only the complimentary copies included with an author's publishing package and then waits to print more as they're ordered—if ever.

The beauty of working with Redbrush is that you can decide how many books you need and how to print them; from a few copies to thousands.

Like most manufacturing, the more of a physical item you produce, the lower the per unit cost. It's the same with books.

Large, traditional publishers use offset printing for most of their printing needs. Offset printing presses use thin aluminum plates that will press ink to a rubber roller or "blanket," then press the ink to paper. You could say this is the standard, old-fashioned way of printing books. It makes great sense if you want to print a lot of books, say a thousand or more. The quality is high and the costs drop pretty quickly once you start printing thousands of copies.

How quickly does that price drop? Here's an example: A church had a book that they gave away to visitors. They gave away about a thousand books every year. So they printed a thousand books every twelve months. By the time I met them, they'd done this twice. The book wasn't going to change, and they wanted another thousand copies. I asked when the book might change. "Maybe in five years, if then."

I suggested they print five thousand copies of the book to save money. They didn't want to print that many copies and spend that much money at one time. I asked if they'd rather spend $12,500 or $4,900. The lower amount, obviously. Then I explained that if they printed five thousand copies of the book for $4,900 (97¢ each), it would cost the same as printing one thousand twice which, remember, they'd already done. Printing five thousand copies was much less expensive than printing one thousand books five times. How much could they save? A little more than $7,500.

Think of it this way. When printing on offset equipment, printing more books takes more paper and ink and a little more time. Presses are so fast that printing higher quantities doesn't require significantly more labor or energy. For this reason, when you are confident you have a need for more books, consider printing them in advance. This lowers your per unit costs and can increase your profit margin substantially.

How much? Let's use that same book that the church gave away. At its current specifications, it could have been sold for about ten dollars each. After all expenses, the profit on each sale would be about $6.50, or $6,500 if they printed and sold a thousand copies a year, or $32,500 in five years.

If they printed five thousand with the lower per unit cost, their profit margin would be about $8.25 a book or $8,250 per one thousand sold. That's $42,500 over five years. Add that $10,000 to the $7,500 of savings, and they've earned $17,500 *more* net profit ($60,000 total) than by printing a thousand books per year for five years.

Do the math and see how much more savings and profit you can realize by thinking more long-term and confidently knowing how many books to print and sell over time.

The digital printing platform is usually more cost-efficient when you need up to a thousand or so copies. Digital printing quality has improved greatly over the years, so much so that it's difficult to tell the difference between it and offset printing with the naked eye. Digital presses use an electric charge to transfer inks or pigments to a roller, then to the paper stock.

Digital printing has become so cost-efficient that it's possible to print individual copies of a book to fulfill single book orders on-demand. This digital method allows for independent publishers to quickly produce and distribute books. This is called Print-On-Demand digital printing, and can be very helpful to indie publishing authors like you. More on that a little later.

I often ask authors how many copies of their book they think they can sell. The answers I receive tell me a lot about the authors and their level of confidence in themselves and their books.

When someone tells me, "oh gosh, I don't think I'll be able to sell more than a hundred copies of this book," they're probably going to be right. Then there's the author who crows, "This is an important book. I've got a great plan in place! I'm going to sell thousands!" They're probably right, too. If you're confident and hoping for the best, you'll find something redeeming in the results.

So, it's no stretch of the imagination that independent publishers who are optimists will succeed better than pessimists. I know it sounds cliché. But if you're a glass-half-empty author, you're going to have a rougher go than the glass-half-full writer.

## Confidence

Redbrush was created to help highly motivated authors indie-publish better books ... and eBooks and audiobooks, and so on. We have pledged to help with the guidance and tools to help you succeed in ways that other publishing options cannot.

Our wish is to help you indie-publish better, smarter, and with better results than you've ever been able to before. We will help you build confidence through knowledge and experience. We know that the more confident you are, the greater your chance of success with your published products.

We want to earn your confidence as you build confidence in yourself and your book.

## Process

When you're ready to place a print order to have books printed and sent to you, we've created an easy production process. You can easily get printing quotes. Once you've hit upon the quote you like, confirm that quote and check over its specifications to make sure everything is the way you want it. Convert that confirmed quote to a Purchase Order, and we'll email it to you to return with your signature.

If we don't already have your files, you'll get them to us through the Internet or on archived media (a flash drive, CD-ROM, or DVD). If we haven't prepared your files, we'll move them to Pre-Flight and check them over to make sure that they meet our Printing Requirements. Again, Pre-Flight is included in the cost of your print job.

Once they've passed Pre-Flight, we'll move files to the printer to get in line for a printed proof to be prepared and sent to you.

You'll receive the proof about a week to ten days from the time your printing job's been moved to the print department. The cost of the proof itself is included in the print job. You are responsible for the cost of shipping the proof. (You can choose to have the printed proof sent more quickly—even Next Day Air for example, if time is an issue—or by ground shipping if lower costs are.)

You'll carefully review your printed proof. This is the last of the checks and balances in place to help insure your book turns out as you expect. If changes need to be made to the files, adjustments can be done at your expense before the print job continues. New, corrected PDF files will be sent to the printer, as needed.

If corrections have been made, you can choose to view another printed proof or to view an electronic proof to be sure that the changes you've requested were made and no other mistakes have been caused or accidentally occurred.

The print order is then moved to the final production queue. The books are printed and bound, then moved to shipping for packaging to ship to you.

Like shipping the proof, the cost of shipping books to you is not included in the quoted printing price. Shipping costs are calculated once the books have been packaged and all variables have been determined (number of cartons, speed of shipping, weight of the total order, and the cost of fuel—a wildly fluctuating variable).

# After Printing

As you think about your publishing process, you'll want to consider what distribution methods will work best for you. Before you choose your distribution plan, you'll need to consider how you'll be selling your book: by direct and/or indirect means.

First and foremost, you'll want to directly sell books yourself—face-to-face and hand-to-hand—to people you meet and who fit in one of your targeted audiences. These will be folks from your booster list: family, friends, business colleagues and coworkers, and every one of the people they personally refer to you.

Second, you can sell books through your own website. If you have bigger goals, you'll want and need to have an appropriate Web presence that includes information about your book and a simple way for folks to purchase it. Plan on selling to folks who hear about you and your book from people who review or endorse it. Hopefully a lot of customers will choose to purchase directly. If you've printed books in advance and don't want to handle the packaging and shipping of books to your customers—and some folks don't want to have any part of that—it's possible to arrange for shipping and fulfillment to send out books to your customers on your behalf. It's efficient and not as costly as you might think.

If you're a speaker who leads conferences, workshops, and similar opportunities to sell books to attendees—or will include copies with event materials—another advantage of a storage and fulfillment program is to move books to your venues so you don't have to. No one wants to carry cartons of books along with them. It's so much easier to have books waiting for you at the engagement.

The best reason to sell books directly to your readers and audiences is that you make *all* the profits on your book sales. You are the publisher. After you've paid for the books and other expenses, you receive the net profits from the sales of your books: 100 percent of the profits are yours.

Indirect sales are any sales that you arrange or allow through a retail partner, distributor, or other sales channel. Just like a big traditional publisher has to allow retail partners to make money on book sales, you'll share some of the profit pie when you allow your customers to buy from other sources. There are great advantages to letting retailers sell your books.

## Distribution: POD + Storage & Fulfillment = Enough

One of the most important developments in the publishing and book printing industries has been the creation of Print-On-Demand (POD) production and distribution programs. Digital print capabilities have evolved to the point where a single book can be printed digitally and quickly distributed to the end user. When the ability to easily add new titles to retailers' distribution lists arrived, it became possible for published works—printed books, eBooks, and other editions—to quickly become available through popular online booksellers, brick-and-mortar bookstores, and virtually any bookseller wanting to sell them.

POD makes it relatively easy for any publisher—especially small and independent publishers—to quickly list available products and begin directing customers to them as they choose. Most of the vanity press publishers utilize POD to streamline production and distribution. Various self-publishing services companies do, too. Redbrush offers POD as a desirable component for many indie book publishers.

Redbrush has created a POD partnership to further streamline the process of moving your title through the distribution channels quickly and efficiently.

## How It Works

Redbrush has created a program to serve our authors' Print-On-Demand needs. We partner with established POD printers so that your books will be listed through the broadest number of retailers, distributors, and sales channels. In addition to over 30,000 channels in the US, you can add retail partners and distributors in Canada, Europe, Australia, India, and the Far East. What this means for you is that if you have customers looking for your book, they can easily find it.

Once print-ready PDF files are completed and ready for printing, we'll move copies of the files to our partner's printing facility to archive in their servers, at the ready for orders that arrive from partnering retail booksellers. You'll receive a sample as a proof before your title goes live. We recommend that when you start seeing your title appear on popular bookselling websites, you order a copy yourself from the site or store of your choice—or have a close friend or family member do so to experience how easy it is for your customers to order books.

Be aware that your book won't show up everywhere at the same time. Because there are so many partnering retailers and distributors involved, and though your title information is broadcast to each of them at the same time, each administers their own distribution lists and sites, so your title will appear when available over a period of a few weeks. Anticipating these stuttered arrivals is helpful.

## Wait For the Starting Gun

One of the most difficult things at this stage of your publishing journey is waiting. Before you reach that point of crowing about your book's availability to purchase, you'll want to be sure that your book is available. The best time to start marketing your title's launch is after you've received books yourself for your direct sales *and* you've seen your book appear on the most popular of the bookselling websites. There might be nothing as damaging to your bookselling success than telling people to buy a book they can't find.

Another reason to wait for these two conditions is credibility. Nothing says "professionally published book" faster than being able to easily find it in the places where people look for and buy book products. More often, that means *online*—either at your site or one familiar to your audiences.

## What about Bookstores?

Physical, brick-and-mortar bookstores are probably not the best primary location to sell your indie book title. Bookstores still sell a lot of books—but almost all of them come from traditional publishers and are backed by a lot of marketing juice (big budgets). You may be able to arrange for your local store to feature your new book in the "Local Author" section—if they have one. If you have a relationship with your local store's manager or buyer and they know you as a customer and not just someone who's peppered them with questions about how to get your book on their shelves, they may be able to give you a little presence somewhere. They might even host a reading or signing event. "Local Author Publishes New Book" is still a popular human interest story in most communities. Maybe they'll be able to help, particularly if they're an independent bookstore and are aware of the painstaking process you've gone through to produce a superior book product. If a bookstore wants to stock your book, Redbrush offers a program to make that easy for your retail bookstore manager and/or buyer.

Think like that bookstore manager or buyer for a moment. They're watching their beloved bookselling industry and store-based book sales change year after year. There's never been enough room for all of the books that the traditional publishers wanted stocked on their shelves. Now there are hundreds of thousands of books from vanity press publishers and more authors than ever walking in wanting to hawk their vanity projects. You might even hear the argument that there are more authors than readers. It sure can seem that way when you're in their shoes.

Many bookstores sell magazines, calendars, movies, music, coffee, and muffins to draw customers in, hoping some will pause long enough to buy a book, too. Many have started selling eBook readers.

If you get a bookstore to stock your book, their desired profit margin can be as high as 65 percent of the retail price of the book. Unless you're printing a couple thousand copies to bring your per unit price down, this doesn't make a lot of sense. Try to negotiate a consignment deal or short term arrangement with no risk to the bookseller, where you'll guarantee to take back any books without question if they don't sell. (This isn't very practical anywhere other than at your local bookstores.)

Just when you thought the prospect of getting your book into stores couldn't be any more difficult, there's another challenge: returnability.

The bookselling industry is a pretty odd bird to most of us customers. It's one of the commercial industries where retailers have the option of returning unsold products in return for credit against future products. Here's how it works. Let's say a traditional publisher—"Simon Collins & Penguin"—has their salesperson visit the store manager or buyer with the next catalog of titles, coming out in several months. Based on the big marketing budgets and promotional plans for each of the titles being presented, the buyer chooses which books they believe customers will be hearing about and coming in to purchase.

Let's use the example of a Harry Potter book by J.K. Rowling. Let's suppose the manager believes their store will sell a thousand copies. The salesperson is going to suggest that the store buy fifteen hundred copies. After all, if the books don't sell, they can be returned to the publisher's distributor, and the store will receive full credit. There is virtually no risk. The bookseller has more than enough copies of a popular release on hand. The publisher's salesperson gets a better sales commission. Those customers who value their bookstore and the experience of buying the book from the store are happy. Win. Win. Win. Right?

But most books are not written by the amazing Ms. Rowling. A manager or buyer will buy some copies of those anticipated bestsellers—they can always order more if something really takes off. They might try a couple copies of other books that catch their eye. There may not be room for more. Those books will sit, spine out, waiting quietly to be wanted by a buyer that's been reached by good marketing or is browsing and looking for exactly that kind of book. Still, there is little risk for the bookseller. After a few months, if they haven't sold, they'll be pulled and shipped back, to be replaced by the next season's hopefuls.

One of the best things about POD distribution is the ability of your customer to walk into virtually any bookstore and ask for the book. It doesn't have to be there. "Sorry, we don't currently have that in stock. But I can get it here in a few days. How many copies would you like?" Sold.

## Exceptional Books Require Exceptional Opportunities

Better books need the best chance to succeed. Redbrush has created a special distribution program that provides exactly the functions that exceptional books need to achieve the greatest successes.

Redbrush's FRS distribution program provides order fulfillment, allows bookstore/retailer returns, and storage solutions to give authors with superior products the better chance to sell books through traditional stores and other partnering resellers. FRS isn't for everyone. In fact, the program is available only to those authors with a superior book and plotted course for success, as determined by Redbrush staff.

## Start Your Engines

Remember, before the Internet, publishers focused exclusively on store and mail-order sales. Just as printing technologies have changed, so have the way publishers sell books. As an indie book publisher, you'll use the smartest marketing and methods to sell more books to your targeted audiences. Using Redbrush, you're able to sell books wherever your customers want to buy them, and that's pretty great!

To get them to buy them, you have to first get your book(s) on your customers' radar. Which leads us to ...

The Compass

# Marketing

## Before, During, and After Printing

This is where it gets fun. Hold on. It's going to get loud!

More than one author has quizzed me, asking, "What is the most difficult part of the publishing process?" My answer?

Writing your manuscript is the most difficult part of the publishing process ... until you get the manuscript done and you've decided to publish it. Then, the preparation and printing are the most difficult step—because you have control and responsibility over many of the steps—until your book's ready, printed, and in your hands. Then, marketing your book is the most difficult part, until you've successfully reached whatever success you can achieve and you're ready to start on the next book. Writing your follow-up manuscript will be most difficult step of your publishing experience.

One of the ways to lighten the load at every step is to always keep your marketing in mind. The best way to do that is to see the publishing process as a cycle, more than a linear process. At Redbrush, we want you to enjoy your indie book publishing experience so much that you'll choose to "Write. Publish. Be Red." and repeat. During the first project you'll cut your teeth and learn the steps and processes to complete a successful publishing voyage. The second project will be easier, as will the next, and the next, and so on.

What makes it all possible—what makes indie book publishing the most practical of your publishing options—is *you*, successfully presenting and selling your books and products to your targeted audiences.

Merriam-Webster defines marketing as "the process or technique of promoting, selling, and distributing a product or service." While Redbrush can help you with each of these functions, it's the promotion of your title that will make the difference in your success and ability to reach your identified goals.

Not every book can be a bestseller. Not every restaurant will survive. Not every movie will be a box office smash or receive critical acclaim—two very different types of success. It can be helpful to know as early as possible if your book will be able to reach the destinations of success that you've identified. One of the simplest ways of thinking about this is imagining a cross-country trip from one coast to the other in your car.

Will your car make it through the plains, over the Rockies, and across the deserts safely? Some of us might be confident enough to jump in and drive. To prepare for such a journey, some will change their car's oil, check the tires, and perform any needed maintenance before taking off.

Redbrush starts with an author intensive discovery process to first identify an author's specific goals and targeted audiences. Redbrush also offers a Book Marketing Appraisal to help authors determine whether their manuscript and subsequent book will be able to get you where they want to go. The appraisal will help authors decide what marketing they can do on their own and what kinds of marketing activities will be most appropriate for the type of book they've written and will be offering in the bookselling marketplace. There's also a helpful combination appraisal that can evaluate the manuscript's editorial integrity. These appraisals can provide great baselines as any author starts their publishing journey.

## Anywhere, Anytime, To Anyone

There are several steps in the publishing continuum: writing, publishing, marketing, succeeding, and repeating. For the writer with a single book project, these steps might be completed in a very linear fashion. When the book's in your hands and you're trying to get it into others', you've arrived at a finish line of sorts. Try to think of every finish line as the starting line for the next task.

When thinking of an author's publishing process, I like the image of a traffic roundabout. We've all seen photos of elaborate statues in the center of a huge, multi-laned roundabout in some far-off European city or larger American metropolis. At the center of smaller roundabouts you might find a flower garden. Still smaller roundabouts sometimes feature a sculpture or a milestone marker.

Each author needs only be concerned with their own roundabout; a quiet, smooth, single-lane path on their own publishing journey. It's small enough so you can confidently see all of your available options and exits, but it's big enough that you have to see each turn off as a distinct and necessary step to complete your journey.

As each of you travels along, you can turn off to start appraisal, editing, or design. Return to the path when your files are ready, then pull off to print books. Once books are ready, you can move to distribute and sell.

Imagine that in the center of your roundabout there is a special, single parking space, alongside an information station—a quaint little kiosk (with great coffee, Wi-Fi, and *reliable* cellular reception). This is your marketing junction. You can stop here at any time during your publishing journey. We encourage you to constantly be aware and drop by throughout your overall process to formulate and initiate marketing processes while your book is underway. It's a great place to stop when you're waiting for editing to be completed … or design, etc.

Because this marketing spot is centrally located, it's easy—anytime you have a moment—to spend a little time fine-tuning your marketing plans and elements, and promoting your book. Social media makes this easy, too. Marketing is an ongoing process, kind of a pulse that needs to beat throughout your publishing cycle(s).

Marketing can be compared to how some sharks breathe. Some shark species breathe by extracting oxygen from the water using ram ventilation, meaning they must stay in motion so that water constantly enters their mouths and passes over their gills. If they're not moving forward, they're not breathing. If they're not breathing, they're dying.

Marketing your independent book is the same way. If you're not moving forward, marketing your book to your audiences, your book's not likely to sell. Quiet books are rarely noticed. Be ready to market and promote your book, yourself, and your overall platform throughout the various stages of your indie book's publishing journey. There are several appropriate ways to market your book before, during, and after its publication. You'll want to choose the best marketing options at the right time for your book. (Obvious example: don't even schedule book launch events before you have books.)

## It's All About the PWOM, Baby!

I quiz authors, "what do you think is the most important element in reaching your publishing goals?" I've already talked about it a couple of times in the previous pages. The answer might not be what you think.

Some authors say the title and/or cover of their book is the most important piece of the success puzzle. No doubt about it; covers and title can attract attention. Your book's visual presentation is definitely important—but not the *most* important.

"Editorial integrity?" Another very important piece of the recipe. Without editorial integrity, you probably won't reach the most important element.

"Credibility?" A well-written, professional-looking product, quality construction, and broad availability certainly lend credibility to your title, and that's a very positive part of the whole.

"Reviews and endorsements from credible people?" Very close! Blurbs and reviews from people you know and people you don't can also be an important element in your book's success and can draw customers to it.

"Positive word of mouth!"

Yes! Even if you don't like the look of that new restaurant—or the funky, spicy smells that come from it—the recommendation from a trusted friend who loved it might get you in the door. When you avoid a film because that *one actor you find annoying* has a major role, a coworker's enthusiasm for the movie might just put you in a theater seat. You might never hear about a new novel in the genre that you love unless a friend gushes about it and you give it a try.

## Show Me the PWOM! (Rhymes with "farm," if you're from Boston.)

Positive word of mouth is the single most important element in your book's success. The tricky thing about the "PWOM" is that you can't create it all yourself. By its very definition, PWOM has to come from others … others who know and like your title. Without satisfied customers, you won't receive referrals. Without readers who love your book, there's no one talking at the water cooler, on the plane as they travel, in the line at the box office, over lunch, or posting online about your book.

Maybe this has happened to you. Think of this like telling a new joke at the office. If the joke "kills" and leaves everyone in stitches, it's going to make the rounds through the office before lunch. If the joke bombs, you could be telling the same joke for weeks and never come across anyone who's heard it before. You *don't* want that to happen to your book.

Readers can be a fickle bunch. Some of them might not feel the love for your cover or dislike how you described the female lead. Some of them might think the rant is inconsistent in your nonfiction manifesto. Prospective customers might or might not be impressed with your reviews, blurbs, or lack thereof. But if their overall impression is positive, they'll be more likely to share information about your book with their circle of friends and influence—especially those they know like the same kind of books. Why?

Everyone loves being in the know. Knowledge is power. Most folks like to help their peers. It makes them feel good when they can share something new with a peer or their circle of friends. Remember the first time you heard about Harry Potter, *The Hunger Games*, or *Fifty Shades of Grey?* Chances are it was someone's recommendation that helped you make the purchase.

I remember the first time I heard about Tom Clancy's *The Hunt for Red October* and Christopher Moore's wildly irreverent storytelling. (Thanks, Dan!) Personal recommendations have introduced me to more great books, authors, films, and music than any other source. I bet that's the case for you, too.

The fact that I could easily find supporting marketing messages about these books didn't hurt. After hearing about a title, reading some online reviews helped. Finding a review in a magazine or newspaper nudged me closer to a purchase. But without the PWOM, that new book or movie or whatever might not have appeared on my radar. PWOM can make all the difference in the world.

A round of smart marketing resulted in a ripple effect that had a provocative, quasi-children's book title on the lips of millions of readers, parents, critics, and … just about everyone. Love it or hate it, *Go the F*ck to Sleep* took the bookselling world by storm not too long ago. Social media helped the title sail to the bestseller lists. Sometimes a little shock value can go a long way. People who hated the book—or even just the idea of it—resulted in sales to the curious. Negative word of mouth is better than silence, but do your best to generate positive word of mouth.

## Social Media

How do you receive PWOM about anything? Folks just don't hover around the water cooler, as they did in the past. These days, a little bird probably tweeted it. You saw a friend's Facebook post.

A colleague or someone else you follow mentioned it on their blog. The same social media methods that caused Grumpy Cat (www. grumpycats.com) to become an online sensation and help all manner of goofy videos and silly posts to go viral in just days can help you reach more readers in your targeted audiences than ever before. (What *does* the fox say?)

Will the professional cover help? Absolutely. Does your book's readability matter? You bet it does. Do blurbs and bits of praise help sell books? Yes, they do. These and other elements contribute to stronger and more frequent PWOM. The more PWOM the better. *¡Viva la PWOM!*

Make PWOM one of your targeted goals. The stronger your product and your marketing, the better and more successful your PWOM will be. The stronger your PWOM, the greater your sales.

## Traditional Marketing

You're not Simon & Schuster, so you don't have to market your products like they do, thank goodness. (Fact is, they're starting to market their books and products exactly as we suggest you should.) Because you're not a big, traditional publisher, you don't have the same level of risk, or investment, or urgency that they do. For the time being, they tie themselves to a calendar of seasons and selling cycles. They must invest tens of thousands of dollars into every book they publish and hundreds of thousands or more for their top tier titles. Traditional marketing is costly, because they have to generate top tier attention and maintain primary position in the customer's mind. Scattergun marketing is costly.

You've probably heard of manuscripts that generate a feeding frenzy and publishing rights that sell for a million dollars or more. Can you imagine the marketing dollars that will have to support a book into which a traditional publisher has already dumped seven figures?

We recommend rifle-shot marketing, firing off information as directly as you possibly can to your targeted readers and audiences.

Your goal should be to reach your identified ideal readers as directly as you can with information and calls to action that lead them to your products or, at very least, your website.

Think of it this way.

You have a book about carving ice sculptures for fun and profit. You contract with the commercial blimp that's shooting overhead shots for one of the big college football stadiums in December. You've got the idea to dump little fliers out of the blimp to gently fall upon the football fans at the end of the game to share the title of your book and to direct people to your website where they can buy it. What could possibly be wrong with this plan?

The Hawaii Bowl holds 50,000 people, and brings fans from around the country to the Islands each winter to enjoy sun and surf, and watch the country's best college players play on Christmas Eve or Christmas Day. How much could 50,000 little sheets of paper cost? This is that scattergun approach at its best and worst.

*Cost is irrelevant if the marketing method won't accomplish what you desire.* You have a world of marketing opportunities and vendors to help you directly reach your targeted audiences. The more clearly you can identify your readers, the easier and more cost-efficient it will be to reach them.

Your title, your audiences, and your goals will wholly define the marketing methods you'll need to consider. Press releases, press kits/electronic press kits, direct marketing mailers, paid advertising spots, Advance Review Copies (ARCs)/Advance Review eBooks (ACEs), blog posts, professional reviews, interviews, book signings, social media campaigns, and more can be part of your marketing plan to reach your identified target audiences. Redbrush can help you determine exactly the marketing plan that makes the best sense for you. For a fee, we can even spearhead the use of these marketing methods on your behalf.

## What About the Ice Sculpting Book?

Traditional marketing methods probably aren't the best way to reach this book's targeted readers—folks who might like to try ice sculpting as a hobby and/or to eventually gain a second income. Could this be a tighter niche market?

What might work better? Why not get in touch with chainsaw dealers or tool distributors who handle ice-carving chisels? Restaurant suppliers might also be the place to reach those interested in trying their hand at sculpting centerpieces for special occasions and holidays. Caterers who do engagement dinners, weddings, anniversary parties, and any sort of social event would be a better place to sell than a tropical sporting event. Reach out to commercial ice vendors who would supply the raw materials.

The National Ice Carvers Association (www.NICA.org) would also be an ideal source of information and databases, to see what other resources are already available and where. Sometimes, finding a related organization, business, or trade association makes the best sense to locate members of your ideal audiences.

## Books with a Beat

Of the thousands of authors I've personally helped and coached over the last decade, few have impacted me more than those whose primary goal is to "make a difference in at least one person's life." There are many ways that indie publishing authors can make a difference, benefit a cause, or pay it forward in big and small ways. I think you'll agree that if even one person's life is impacted; if even one child's outlook is brightened; if a community can be helped through a time of challenge, it's worthwhile to do what you can. Here's how to give your book project a heartbeat.

Some authors build books for the sole purpose of donating their proceeds to a specific nonprofit cause or organization. They may choose to pay themselves back for their publishing expenses or they may write them off as business expenses and then donate their profits from sales to an organization relevant to their book. They often note on their website and in their books that "a portion of proceeds from the sale of this book will be donated to ..."

You can choose whether or not to name a specific organization or percentage to be donated on your book. I recommend that you keep the specifics somewhat vague for two important reasons. First, one never knows what experience others have had with a given cause or organization. You never want to give someone a reason *not* to buy your book. Noting an organization that's out of favor with a member of your audience might cost you a sale. Also, what if your feelings change about that organization or you become aware of another group that might better benefit from your donation? A general notation of support on your book allows you the freedom to do as you wish with your donations.

## Donating Books

One of your best sales options is to make volume sales as attractive as possible. If you have a children's book, a business book, or a book that has broad appeal, you may be able to generate greater sales by offering volume discounts. Promote donations to your customer's local or school library by offering a donation copy when customers make a volume purchase. Or, give them the option of having you donate a copy in the customer's name to a library, hospital, care facility, Boys & Girls Club, or relative organization if the customer chooses.

## Heirloom Editions

I've long suggested that author/publishers find ways to pay it forward and help nonprofits or associations that might be relevant to their title. Think of it as "golden rule" or karmic marketing. When you give to others, you'll likely receive something in return. You never know what impact your actions might have. The right gift might yield huge dividends in ways that you cannot imagine. It's worth the costs, and you'll feel great, too. One of the easiest ways to help is by creating and donating heirloom editions of your book. What's an "heirloom edition?"

You might have a novel, a children's book, a poetry collection, or a nonfiction title. Take some of the first printed copies of your book, and sign and number them … "1/25," "2/25," "3/25," for example, and so on—just like an artist does with artist's proofs. If you have an illustrator or a photographer who's participated in the creation of your book, have them sign the copies too. (You might choose to give them a few of these copies as a perk for collaborating with you.) Perhaps there is a special inscription you want to write in each of these special copies. Think of something that really sets them apart from other copies and inscriptions you'll write in the future. Write a placard of information about the book, your goal for it, and how this is a special heirloom edition so that "sale of this book will benefit ..." Donate one or more of these heirloom copies to benefit a couple relative organizations—maybe ones that have a donor dinner and silent auction as part of their year's activities.

The nice thing about these donor auctions is that your product arrives with built-in exclusivity, even—dare I say—collectability! Who knows if you and your book might be the next big thing? Egos jump in. Steve bids against Jane, who bids against Joe, who wants to beat out Hilary—not solely because the book is worthy of big bucks (yet), but because each wants to donate the most.

These auctioned books can sell for hundreds of dollars, benefiting the chosen nonprofit or community program. The organization gets the money. You get the bragging rights. This makes for priceless marketing information on your site, a celebration blog post. It reinforces the exclusivity and collectability of your additional heirloom editions and generates interest in your title.

Whether you choose to offer all of your heirloom editions to organizations or wish to sell some of them to those who want a special signed and numbered edition (at a higher price)—or you want to give them to your boosters and benefactors—you've got something unique and different to promote your title in the marketplace.

## Ask For Support

If there is a special cause relevant to your book, story, or characters in your novel, and members of your target audience are also interested in that cause, consider what organizations might help cross-promote your book. Does an organization have an online newsletter or blog that could feature a review of your book? Would you provide that organization with a donation for every copy they help you sell to their constituency? In anticipation of an organizational event or conference, would they be interested in purchasing a volume of books at a special discount to give or sell to their attendees? Are there corporate sponsors who might pay for a special printing or volume order on behalf of a nonprofit they support? If you have the right book with an appropriate message, you will find never-ending opportunities to promote it to related organizations and their members who might also be your ideal readers.

# Technical Stuff

There are a couple lessons you'll learn during any publishing journey: "you don't know what you don't know," and "what you don't know can cost you." It's up to you whether you learn these lessons right now or let them smack you in the head later … and taint your overall experience forever.

Why are the technical details important? Because what you don't know can cost you in so many ways. If an author/publisher doesn't keep an eye on the technical details:

- They could spend four times what's necessary when they print books.
- They could produce a book that tires the eyes of their readers, so that they put it down sooner and return to it less.
- They could end up with white stripes on the book's cover.
- Their spine's text could end up printing on a fold or on the cover.
- Their children's book illustrations might end up with the gutter over important action or text.
- The bright blood red color of the cover illustration might be dulled to a brownish burgundy by the matte finish they've demanded.
- They might end up with books printed with their name misspelled on the title page or their loved one's name misspelled in the dedication.

Each of these mistakes has affected an author with whom I or a colleague has worked. Each of these mistakes could have been avoided—and some of them would have been—if the author had followed recommendations from their navigator or title manager.

Because the technical details might seem the most challenging, readers sometimes glance over them—with full intention to return and read them carefully later. I can't encourage you strongly enough to take the time to read them carefully. If not now, bookmark the page and come back soon. The more you know and understand about your publishing voyage, the more confident you'll be. The more confident you are, the more successful you'll be—and the more money and embarrassment you can save.

I'll group this information in the form of a Glossary and Frequently Asked Questions (FAQs).

# Glossary, FAQs, and Much, Much More

**B. O. Y. G.** – "Based on your goals." Every product or service that you consider including in your publishing process must be "based on your goals." If you're a highly motivated author with goals of making a significant splash with your book, you'll need to consider higher levels of service and help to reach these higher goals. If yours is a "bucket list" project with the primary goal being to produce a physical product so you can move onto your next list item, you can anticipate a less-involved process and a smaller budget to complete your book.

**B. Y. O. G.** – "Bring your own goals." It's important that you have or can eventually identify the goals that are important for your book publishing project. The more clearly you can define who your targeted audiences are and what you want to accomplish with your book, the more likely you'll be able to successfully reach those audiences and meet those goals. Redbrush provides an in-depth discovery process to help any author and/or team identify their targeted audiences and goals.

**BISAC codes** – The "Book Industry Standards and Communications" codes—sometimes called the "Book Industry Subject and Categories" codes—are numbers assigned to books to categorize them for distributors, libraries, and retail booksellers. Some distributors require them, so it's a good idea to determine which codes best fit your book. You can choose the most appropriate

BISAC codes by going to the Book Industry Standards and Communications site (Current BISAC Subject Headings List at www.bisg.org) or by looking at books similar to yours, to see what codes they chose. (These are updated each year or so. Check the site for the current codes.)

**Black & White (B/W)** - Black and white printing is often referred to as single-color printing, though this might also refer to printing with a single colored ink, too. In this case, white is not a printed color, but an absence of printed ink. It's possible to print percentages of black to create hundreds of shades of gray. Photography and illustrations—even text—can be printed in black and white or grayscale reproduction. In the case of memoirs or other nonfiction books requiring photographic reproduction, b/w is often quite sufficient and most cost-efficient, too.

**Bleed** – When a background or image must print all the way to the edge of a page or cover, it *bleeds* to that edge. When that page or cover is printed, one must allow for the possibility of print variance, an allowance of extra space beyond the trim size's dimension in the event of slight press shift during printing. The image is a little larger than the anticipated trim size to allow for this possibility. This extra bit of printed margin is the *bleed*. It's most often going to be 1/8" when printing must go to the edge.

**CMYK** – Four-color printing is completed by mixing four colors in minute dot patterns on a printed stock. Cyan, magenta, yellow, and black can be mixed to yield millions of color combinations. This is also referred to as full-color printing. Keep in mind that colors on your computer's screen are created by mixing red, green, and blue to create the appearance of different colors. Colors presented in this way, "RGB" color mixing, will be slightly different than CMYK colors. For this reason, it's very important to anticipate slight variances from screen colors to printed colors. This makes the approval of printed proofs all the more important. You'll want to be sure all full-color files that you provide to designers or include in your own PDF files for book covers and interiors are in CMYK color mode, *not* RGB.

**CPSIA** – The Consumer Product Safety Improvement Act (2008) was enacted in response to concerns about the presence of lead and other heavy metals in products manufactured for use by children and imported to the United States. All manufacturers were required to regulate the presence of these metals. American book printers were among the first and fastest industries to comply voluntarily, before the deadlines. As of 2011, book manufacturing was exempt from these regulations. Though CPSIA compliance is no longer required for book manufacturing, some retailers and parental groups still value the presence of compliance notations in book products they sell intended for children. All of Redbrush's manufacturers and partners are CPSIA-compliant. We can instruct you how to note this information in your book, if you so desire.

**Copyright** – Though your writing and other intellectual properties are automatically protected as soon as you take fingers to keyboard or pen to paper, it's advisable to protect physical or shared copies of your work with a copyright symbol (©) and the year of creation. It's possible to register a formal copyright on your work with the US Library of Congress. The copyright lasts from the time the work is created and extends for seventy years after the copyright owner's death. In the event of multiple authors, the copyright extends seventy years following the last surviving author's death. (Visit their website at www.copyright.gov.)

**EAN Bookland barcode** – The EAN Bookland portion of your back cover's ISBN barcode is used to designate the retail price of the printed book. This portion of the barcode indicates the country currency—"5" is used for US Dollars; "6" is used for Canadian Dollars; "0" is used to indicate a price in British Sterling—and the price of the book. In the following examples, the EAN Bookland portion in #1 correctly shows the price to be $29.95 in US Dollars. Example #2 has the EAN Bookland portion with the barcode coded for $4.95 in Canadian Dollars. In example #3, this EAN barcode shows that a retail price has not been designated. It doesn't mean the book is free, just that the publisher hasn't elected to specify a retail price in the barcode. This can be confusing to customers who know how to read them. It's a good idea to set a price and code it into your EAN barcode.

#1 ISBN 978-0-07-575212-7

#2 ISBN 978-0-96-6225730

#3

The font used for the numbers and letters will vary. It's the lines that must be clear so as to be properly scanned as needed. Be sure to leave room for the barcode and space around it, typically 1.25" tall x 2.125" wide.

**Electronic proof** – When design files have been completed—and sometimes before they've been finished—an author/publisher will have the opportunity to view the files as an electronic proof—in PDF form—to view the progress or results of the work that's been completed. During the printing process, sometimes an electronic proof can be viewed to confirm that specific corrections have been made correctly and that the rest of the files have not been affected or otherwise compromised. Any mistakes remaining after final approval, made either by the author or designer, are the sole responsibility of the author.

**.ePub** – eBooks are published in several languages and formats. .ePub is a popular eBook format that is legible by the Nook, Kobo, and other popular eBook reading apps. Most computers and e-readers can download free reader software to read .ePub.

**Fonts** – We western readers grew up printing our letters with little "hats and feet," or serifs. Due to this early programming, our brains are trained to read fonts with serifs easier and for longer periods of time without tiring. Though Times New Roman might be the default font in your word processing program—and it's great for short files/texts and business applications—it's narrower than typical publishing body text fonts. When you're ready to really see how your text might look in a published book, try one of the Garamond or other fonts with serifs. These fonts are designed to be easier to read for long periods of time.

**Four-color** – or "Full-color," refers to the color printing process of combining four colors (CMYK) to create millions of colors.

**Full-color** – or "Four-color," refers to the color printing process of combining four colors (CMYK) to create millions of colors.

**ISBN** – A 10- or 13-digit number assigned to aid in identification of a specific edition of a published title. Assigned by the publisher of the book or product, it also designates who the publisher is— who holds the printing and publishing rights to the work. Because only a publisher can assign an ISBN, it's important to decide if you will independently be your own publisher or use the ISBN of another publisher who will be entitled to decide how sales' profits will be divided. The ISBN usually appears on the copyright page of a printed or electronic book. It can also be coded into a graphical barcode and placed on the back cover of the printed book for easy scanning. eBook editions do not require ISBN barcodes. ISBNs are purchased from the designated ISBN administrator in your country of citizenship— in the US, it's R.R. Bowker—or an allowed vendor.

**ISBN barcode** – While the ISBN usually appears on the copyright page of a printed or electronic book, printed copies of the book also have the ISBN coded in the form of a graphical barcode that's placed on the back cover of the book for easy scanning. Consider this one of the elements that makes an independently published book look like any traditionally published book. Barcodes are inexpensive and provide visual credibility to the product.

**LCCN** – The Library of Congress Control Number is assigned by the US Library of Congress to be printed in books that it is likely to acquire and that other libraries may consider for their collections. Only US book publishers may obtain an LCCN. They must be willing to list the LCCN on the copyright page of the book and maintain an official office that's able to respond to bibliographic questions. If you hope to market your book to libraries, the LCCN is something to consider for your title. LCCN assignment is free. Contact the US Library of Congress at www.loc.gov.

**Margins** – When you type your manuscript, you can use any margin you want. Most writers choose a 1" margin on a standard 8.5x11 sheet. The margins in your printed book should be formatted to publishing industry standards. These can vary depending on the type and trim size of your book. Allow a minimum of .5" around the outside edges and .75" in the gutter to allow extra room for the binding. Due to the possibility of slight print variance, you never want to have text or graphical elements closer than .25" to the edge of your page, anywhere in your book—unless you intend images to fully bleed.

**.mobi** – eBooks are published in several languages and formats. .mobi is the language of Amazon's popular Kindle readers. Most computers and e-readers can download free reader software to be able to read .mobi files.

**Overs/Unders** – In commercial book printing, high-speed presses are able to print books very quickly. Anytime presses or offset plates are used, there is the opportunity for spoilage to occur (smudges, streaks, and other related press-related errors). Book printers typically anticipate spoilage and print extra copies to allow for this. Many commercial printers require that a customer accept either 10 percent over or under the desired print quantity for the job to be considered complete. (Customers only pay for the quantity they receive.) Redbrush asks that author/publisher customers accept no more than 5 percent overs or unders than their desired order quantity. You have the option of requesting and purchasing any additional overrun copies—if they are available—at the same per unit cost as the ordered quantity.

**Page** – A page is one side of a sheet or leaf of paper, bound in a book. This can sometimes be confusing as some commercial printers (not as familiar with trade book printing) will confuse single page printing with sheet printing when printing on only one side. It's helpful to know that book pages are created by folding large sheets or roll-fed paper that's cut down to yield four large sheets, folded in half and trimmed to create a sixteen page signature. Most print pricing will be in increments of these sixteen-page signatures. Some book printing quotes—for short full-color books, for example—can be quoted in eight-page half-signatures.

**PDF files (Portable Delivery Format files)** – PDFs are created to safely move print-ready files to the printer so that books may be printed. When correctly created and saved, PDF files lock in the fonts, graphics, color information, and all of the formatting in an un-editable version so that book can be printed without the introduction of mistakes during the printing phase.

**POD** – Print-On-Demand is a printing method utilizing digital printing presses capable of cost-efficiently producing a single copy of a book at a time. When added to a distribution program or process, POD provides authors/publishers with an affordable method of title distribution and timely delivery of printed books when orders are received. POD is a desirable component for most indie book publishers to consider.

**Printed Proof** – The best way to proof one's design files or book. PDF files are used to create printed proofs and typically output from digital printing or reproduction equipment. They provide the closest and best physical example to proof, short of final press checks—that are seldom practical with trade book printing. Whether the author/publisher receives a printed proof or an electronic proof, it's up to them to carefully review and approve the files before production or next steps can commence. Any mistakes remaining after final approval, made either by the author or designer, are the sole responsibility of the author.

**Ransom** – After an author pays for a vanity press publisher's publishing package that includes design of the print-ready files to print books, they often learn that they—the author—don't own the print-ready files they paid to have created. Should they ever want to break up with that publisher and take their book elsewhere, they'll pay a fee to liberate the book's files. This can sure feel like a ransom when one's paid a lot of money to get a book to market, but can't take it elsewhere without having to start over and have files re-designed or pay required file fees. Oftentimes, there are publisher-specific notations to be removed or corrected before these files are ready to use again, adding costs beyond the ransom.

**RGB** – Also called "three-color process." This type of color reproduction is accomplished by mixing three colors in minute dot patterns on a printed stock or screen. Red, green, and blue inks can be combined to create thousands of colors. Screen color reproduction is RGB, so what one sees on a computer monitor can differ from what's received out of a printing press. For this reason, it's very important to anticipate slight variances from screen colors to printed colors. This makes the approval of printed proofs all the more important. You'll want to be sure all full-color files that you provide to designers or include in your own PDF files for book covers and interiors are in CMYK color mode.

**Shipping** – Shipping costs are fees for delivering books from the printer's dock to the address(es) selected by the author/publisher. This may be a residence, business address, with or without a loading dock, or a distributor's warehouse or storage facility. Depending on the quantity of books and packages being shipped, there may be shipping variables to consider, like speed of delivery, method (commercial carrier vs. OTR), etc. Shipping costs are in addition to printing and production costs. Printing quotes will NOT include shipping costs. Exact shipping costs may not be known until the books are packaged and we're aware of the number of cartons, weight of the order, desired delivery speed and method, etc.

**Signature** – A grouping of sixteen pages, created by folding large sheets or roll-fed paper that's cut down to yield four large sheets, then folded in half and trimmed. Most print pricing will be in increments of sixteen-page signatures. Some book printing—for short children's books, for example—can be quoted in eight-page half-signatures.

**Trim Size** – The dimensions of a book designate the trim size. There are several standard trim sizes that have been established in trade book and children's book publishing. Trim sizes are noted by width first, followed by the height of the book. An "8x10" trim size is eight inches wide and ten inches tall. When a book is bound with a case-wrap hardcover shell, the shell is slightly larger than the interior's finished trim size. These hardcover books are still referred to as "8x10", though the hardcover shell is larger than 8x10.

**Watermarks** – Though the author/publisher owns all rights to the published material, our design teams may add watermarks to all electronic proofs and some printed proofs as a security method until all design work is approved and fully paid. This protects your files from unauthorized use. Anytime special printer pricing or service packaging has been agreed to, proof PDF files may contain watermarks until printing is complete and payments have been received and cleared. Archive PDF files will not have watermarks.

**How much will this cost?** The cost of independently publishing one's own book is determined by the services and processes to be completed to reach the author's identified goals for the project. Building a published book might be somewhat similar to standing on a vacant lot and asking a building contractor how much it will cost to "build a house." Without having the clearest vision of the product, its function(s), and what's to be accomplished by publishing, it can be difficult to estimate what the costs and profits will be. Let us know what you plan to accomplish, and we'll help you get the clearest understanding of the costs involved.

**How long will this take?** Similar question, similar answer. In most cases, the higher the goals and expectations for a book's success, the longer the process will take. Indie book publishing through Redbrush can take as little as a couple weeks and as long as a year, depending on the steps necessary to complete the book that's envisioned by the author/publisher. The most common length of time is about ninety days.

**What's my role?** You are the captain of your publishing voyage. We are your navigator and your crew, aboard to help you reach the desired destination. Because you are your own publisher and will retain all rights and control of your book—and earn the publisher's profits from every sale of it—you will be the leader of this adventure.

**What kind of publishing is this?** Redbrush's model is an independent publishing model, or "indie publishing," as we like to call it. Let's break the publishing models down here again. There's a traditional publishing model, where a company like Random House pays you for the rights to your writing and/or pays you a small royalty when the book they've published sells. They take on the most risk and they make the most money when your book sells. There's the vanity press publishing model, where you pay a publisher to be the publisher of your book and you pay for all of the publishing steps and processes. The vanity press publisher takes the publisher's portion of the profits when/if books sell, and they pay a small portion of each sale's profits to the author when/if books sell. You take all of the risk and have a chance to earn a little of the profit. In Redbrush's indie publishing model, you pay for the services to publish your book. You retain all rights and control of the book, so when sales occur, you receive the publisher's profits from the sales. You've again taken on most of the risk, but you have the best chance of making your money back and building greater success over time.

**What makes Redbrush the best choice for me?** You and you alone can determine if Redbrush is the right fit for your project. If you describe yourself as a highly motivated author committed to independently publishing and building the best success for it, there's no better choice than Redbrush to help you reach your targeted audiences and goals. Redbrush equips its indie publishing authors with exactly the tools and services they need to successfully reach exactly the milestones of success they've identified and their identified ideal readers. No one helps the author champion their own book better than Redbrush.

**What makes Redbrush unique?** Redbrush is the result of over sixty combined years of experience and excellence in the creative and publishing fields. By joining three expert and complementing teams specializing in publishing, printing, social media marketing, and Web design, Redbrush offers the best services to its indie publishing authors, to help re-imagine the stigmatized self-publishing industry into a vibrant and revitalized indie publishing powerhouse.

**What else is better?** How author-publishers pay for their publishing process is different at Redbrush. You get to decide how you want to pay for your publishing process and the services we provide. You can choose to pay-as-you-go for the services you need as you start them. If you're anticipating a specific set of services, you can choose a monthly payment plan to more easily budget your publishing project. You may choose to write a single check for the anticipated total costs for your publishing project. Highly motivated author-publishers are able to plan for their publishing process and journey. We reward you by allowing you to budget smartly at every step.

**If I publish with Redbrush's help, who gets the profits from book sales?** You do. Retailers who help you sell books are entitled to some of the profits, too. That's only fair. We hope you'll tell others about Redbrush, so we can help them with their projects, too. This is how we build success after helping you publish your book and reach your destination.

**So who's the publisher if I publish with Redbrush's help?** You are.

**Who owns the rights to my book?** You do.

**Who owns the ISBN(s)?** You do.

**Who owns the printer files that are designed to print my book?** You do.

**What's the catch?** We want your first born child. (Just kidding. We've got our own rug rats, er ... *little darlings* to take care of!) There is no catch!

# A Few More Nuggets

## How Many Copies Does Each Reader/Customer Need?

Think about customer behavior for a moment. When a customer browses in the bookstore, they might have arrived with no particular book in mind, nothing much on the radar. They may find something that catches their eye and buy a copy. They might just as easily walk out with a calendar and a latte instead of a book. As they browse, the question in their consumer brain may be cycling between "this" or "that?"

If they went in looking for a book on real estate investing, they'll arrive at that section to find a handful of titles. Again, they'll ask themselves, "this or that?" If there are several books on the same topic, they'll probably assume—whether correctly or not—that they all have basically the same information. The customer will compare thickness and price, probably settling on a mid-priced title—one with a sharp cover.

When a customer hears about your book and visits your website or even your book on another online retail site, they're already predisposed to liking your book. You led them to the cover and the title information about it. At this point, the question in their brain is simply, "yes or no?" If the cover is pretty good and the text on the back doesn't turn them off and make them yawn, you have a pretty good chance of making the sale.

Can you manage to draw your prospect to your website and change up the question in their brain from "yes or no?" to "how many?" If so, you have the greater chance of selling at least a single copy. This is called "assuming the sale." Let's use a children's book as the example and assume they've decided they like what they see well enough to buy at least one copy of your title.

What child doesn't have a best friend or two who will also LOVE your book? What child doesn't have a friend with a parent who would love to find another children's book to share with their kid? What child doesn't have a friend or three with a birthday party coming up in the next several weeks? What if there was a volume discount on a "best friends/birthday/cousin/library" option? Add an attractive volume discount that starts with the second book (free shipping!), or a donation copy (for their school or public library) when they purchase more copies, and you'll always be able to drive copy sales. Changing up the question from "this or that?" to "how many?" has never been easier!

## Funding Your Indie Book Project

If you don't have the funds to pay for your publishing journey yourself, consider a funding option like Kickstarter (www.kickstarter.com), GoFundMe (www.gofundme.com), or IndieGoGo (www.indiegogo.com). People who frequent these sites LOVE indie-spirited projects like yours. One of the best reasons to try this type of funding is that your supporters will naturally be members of your target audience. They and their colleagues are predisposed to liking your book and supporting its fundraising campaign. You'll have a built-in audience of folks who will receive copies and you'll have funds available to start or subsidize your own cash.

These funding options require you to put together quality messaging and information for your prospective supporters. They provide great practice talking about and promoting your book. The more easily information about your book and goals rolls off your tongue or out of your fingers, the easier your marketing processes and promotions will go, too, after the book is published. It's a great way to know how many copies you'll need for supporters and extras to sell directly.

## Support Each Other

Chances are you aren't the first person to have written on your nonfiction topic or woven a story about your type of characters. Maybe your collection of poetry will resonate and inspire other poets. Ask other authors for their support. Be aware of other independently published authors in your or related genres and reward satisfying books with positive reviews online. If you blog, review the competition and promote books that help you build organic SEO results while floating all boats. Reach out to them and build community. Provide links to their book or site on yours. Invite those authors to review your title on their site. You might even pick a friendly fight if your views differ. Even controversy can benefit both titles if you can draw people to your discussion and involve them in the debate.

You'll find that by opening dialogue with other authors or about other books, you'll draw their readers to your book and complement their experience with other books on the subject or in a similar genre.

## Build Interactivity

Give your readers a reason to return to your website and title again and again. Engaging and imaginative blog posts are a great way to involve your readers and customers with your website. Offering visitors the first chapter of your next book, a free short story, or similar freebies is a great way to build your audience. Offer paid customers a free eBook download if they come to your site and request it. Post interviews. Announce book signings. Allow comments or feedback about your book or posts. Allow them to "Like" your title/site/posts/announcements on their social media of choice, to promote you to their friends and colleagues. The more often you can generate return visitors to your site, the more likely they'll invite others.

Think "community" as you spread word of your book and its related ideas and topics, and you'll build additional sales while others sit quietly … "out there," waiting to be stumbled upon.

## Bookstore Availability vs. Placement

Bookstore placement is not the same thing as bookstore availability. You want folks to be able to order your book from their local bookstore—if they choose. You want your local bookstore to be able to order additional copies for placement on shelves if they choose. Wrestling to have a copy or two of your book on the shelf to compete alongside the thousands of traditionally published titles there—hoping for an impulse sale—is not the best use of your marketing energy.

Most customers are perfectly happy ordering a book they want from their local store or an online retailer. If you've done your marketing work well, you're focusing on your targeted audiences, who are much more likely to appreciate your information and presentation, and buy a copy of your book from you directly, or order from the retailer of their choice.

Focus on direct sales at the start to see if your book finds its audience, receives positive word of mouth, and builds more sales. Once you've established some sales and are ready to prove to bookstore managers that your book may be good enough to warrant consideration, that's the time to consider other traditional ways to distribute your book to bookstores and other retail options. Redbrush can help with a program that helps those retail booksellers stock your book if they choose.

# Redbrush

## Book Project
## Case Studies

**Project 1**
**A Calling Card Book**

**Project 2**
**A Children's Picture Book**

## Project 1
## A Calling Card Book

Jan has a new manuscript of 50,000 words for a book to support her life coaching presentations. She facilitates workshops twice a month to groups of one hundred to 250 participants. Her book complements her workshop themes perfectly and contains additional information so that participants purchase it following her events.

From start to finish, Jan might expect the following services and costs:

**Editorial & Book Marketing Appraisal**                              **$249.00**
    A general appraisal of both the editorial integrity of the manuscript and the overall viability of the book as a commercial product with recommendations to effectively present and market the book and related editions.

---

**Level 2 Edit**                                            $0.035/word or
    Mechanical editing plus basic sentence structure.        **$1750.00**

---

**Cover and Interior Design**                                   **$1100.00**
    Customized from a concept provided by the author.
    Fully customized design with interior figures and illustrations.

---

**eBook Design**                                               **$500.00**
    In .mobi and .ePub formats for Kindle, Nook, Kobo, Mac, and more.

---

**Printing (Anticipating a 256-page paperback book)**        $1.85 each or
    5000 paperback copies for use at workshops, to         **$9250.00**
    share with media and inquirers as a calling card.

---

**Shipping**                              **Varies depending upon location.**

---

**Marketing/Launch assistance**                                **$1500.00**
    Consultation for book launch, design support, social media setup and coaching.

---

**Distribution**                                               **$1050/yr.**
    FRS (Fulfillment/Bookstore Returnability/Storage) package
    Setup for Print-On-Demand for 38,000 retail partners

---

**ISBNs (a block of ten)**                                      **$295.00**

---

**Total, as described**                                      **$15,694.00***

Jan priced her book at $19.95 to herald its high value. If she sells 4000 copies at a direct-to-reader discount of $10.00, she'll receive $40,000. Jan chooses to sell the eBook versions of the book for $9.99.

# Project 2
## A Children's Picture Book

Tom and Pam have a paperback children's book to help children anticipate and enjoy their first flight in a real airplane. Their illustrations are complete and the book will be laid out in twenty-four pages. The pair will market their book through parenting and travel blogs, travel agents, airports, and schools.

From beginning to end, Tom and Pam might expect the following services and costs:

**Children's Book Appraisal**                                   **$219.00**
A general appraisal of both the editorial integrity of the manuscript and the overall viability of the book as a commercial product with recommendations to effectively present and market the book and related editions.

**Children's Book Edit**                                        **$400.00**
Mechanical editing plus editing for age-appropriate language.

**Cover and Interior Design**                                   **$650.00**
Customized from a concept provided by the author.

**eBook Design**                                                **$500.00**
In .mobi and .ePub formats for Kindle, Nook, Kobo, Mac, and more.

**Printing**                                            $2.00 each or
3000 copies to share with media, sell through their     **$6000.00**
own site, through retailers, and at events for the first two years.

**Shipping**                              **Varies depending upon location.**

**Marketing/Launch assistance**                                 **$1500.00**
Consultation for book launch, design support, social media setup, best practices to sell to libraries and schools, and coaching.

**ISBNs (a block of ten)**                                      **$295.00**

**Total, as described**                                         **$9,564.00***

Tom and Pam have priced their paperback children's book at $14.95. If they sell 2,000 copies at a direct-to-reader discount of $10.00, through their own site, they'll realize sales of $20,000. If they sell 1000 through distributors and retailers for a wholesale price of $5.00 each, they'll earn another $5,000. They price the eBook editions at $7.99, prompting more direct paperback sales, but not losing eBook sales.

# *Redbrush*

# Book Project
# Case Studies

Redbrush provides these case studies to help authors envision what kind of steps, services, and costs should be anticipated in their indie publishing project.

Not all projects require the comprehensive services noted here. Some require more editing, custom design, or marketing consulting to achieve the best published product the author can produce. The more closely the published book fits the needs and expectations of identified, target audiences, the greater the likelihood that it will succeed in reaching the desired goals of its author through greater sales.

For the clearest view of the services and costs appropriate for your book project, please consult a member of the Redbrush team.

For those authors indie publishing as part of a business venture or entrepreneurial project, there may be significant tax benefits available. Be sure to confer with your tax preparer or accountant to take advantage of the appropriate deductions or benefits for your publishing business expenses.

*Remember, all pricing is valid at press time. Costs for items not sold by Redbrush are also subject to change.*

**Redbrush**
1201 Infinity Court
Lincoln, NE 68512
Toll-free: 855.379.6218

## Write. Publish. Be Red.

# Head RED

Hopefully, you've read through *The Compass* and found it helpful as you consider what future success you want for your book. Whether you want something to pass around to your family and loved ones at the next holiday get-together, hope to intrigue new audiences with your creative writings, or aim to present a competent, credible product to colleagues and customers, you now have a clearer idea of who you want to reach and what you want to put in their hands. You have identified what success you desire for your book and have a better view on how to reach that destination.

As you read these last paragraphs, you've hopefully already determined what publishing option will provide the best and most confident path to reach your audiences and goals. You know the difference between the traditional publishing model, the vanity press publishing model of paying someone else to be your publisher, and indie-publishing your book yourself. You understand the importance of who owns your title's ISBNs, controls the printing and publishing rights, and who will make the most money when your book sells. It can be *you*.

You've come to realize that if you have the desire, the drive, and the wherewithal, you can bring your book to market smarter, better, and faster than most of the so-called "self-published" books—and certainly those from the vanity press publishing model.

*The Compass* has also introduced you to Redbrush, a different kind of publishing services provider. We can help you publish your book with the highest editorial integrity, as visually pleasing as anything on the market, and available through the broadest and most cost-efficient distribution channels.

We want to work with authors, artists, storytellers, illustrators, and small publishers who are motivated to confidently hold the wheel and steer their own projects, to reach whatever successful shores they desire. Redbrush can provide expert navigation, a professional team to crew your voyage, and services to give you the best chance to reach your identified goals and destination.

Of course, you don't have to set your sights on world domination or cracking some "bestseller" list to want to put out a professional book product. If your desire is to simply, competently publish your book and let it prove itself—quietly or fiercely—Redbrush is the partner for you.

When you're ready, we're ready.

The charts are open. *The Compass* has revealed true north. The sails are hungry. Shall we cast off, Captain?

# The Red Lists

## Redbrush's Basic, 10-Step Checklist for Any Project

Here's a quick checklist to consider as you start your publishing voyage.

- ☐ Complete your manuscript
- ☐ Complete the Redbrush Indie-Publishing Questionnaire
- ☐ Editing
- ☐ Decide whether to pursue Reviews/Endorsements
- ☐ Buy ISBN(s) and apply for LCCN/PCN, as desired
- ☐ Design
- ☐ Marketing Plan for launch
- ☐ Book Printing
- ☐ Distribution
- ☐ Marketing for launch and after launch ("There's no such thing as a free launch.")

## Redbrush's Practical Indie-Publishing Checklist for the Highly Motivated Author

If your desire is to be a fire-starter, then you'll want to anticipate a more comprehensive process and a greater number of steps. They should include:

- ☐ Complete the last draft of your manuscript.
- ☐ Change up your manuscript's appearance and thoroughly proof it and all related, support copy.

- ☐ Decide if you want to do an Editorial and/or Book Marketing Appraisal(s).
- ☐ Complete the Redbrush Indie Book Publishing Discovery Questionnaire.
  - a. Identify your book's "ideal reader."
  - b. Determine your book's top five target audiences.
  - c. Decide when you'll register a formal copyright for your work.
  - d. Decide if ARCs are desired and, if so, what short list of contacts and reviewers will be contacted about providing reviews and/or endorsements.
  - e. Determine the desired book launch date.
- ☐ Complete Editorial and/or Book Marketing Review(s).
- ☐ Determine the number of necessary ISBNs for the anticipated editions of your book project and purchase the ISBNs from R.R. Bowker.
- ☐ Consider what editorial changes and marketing processes are most appropriate for your book.
- ☐ Choose and purchase the desired level of Editorial Services (Editing).
- ☐ Commence with Book Marketing Services.
- ☐ Complete professional editing.
- ☐ Implement editing changes and thoroughly proof the manuscript.
- ☐ Complete the Indie Book Design Questionnaire.
- ☐ Complete desired professional book design.
- ☐ Thoroughly proof the completed design files.
- ☐ Generate book quotes and determine the best quantity.
- ☐ Submit purchase order for book printing.
- ☐ Have print-ready files moved to printer and Pre-Flight as needed.
- ☐ Receive and thoroughly proof the printed proof.
- ☐ Approve for printing or request necessary corrections.
  - a. Receive and thoroughly proof the electronic proof.
  - b. Approve for printing.

- ☐ Receive shipped books and/or have some moved to distribution.
  a. Initiate POD production and distribution program.
- ☐ Commence with Book Marketing Launch activities.
- ☐ Prepare post-launch Book Marketing Plan.
- ☐ Continue with post-launch Book Marketing Plan and maintenance.

# Notes

# Notes

www.ingramcontent.com/pod-product-compliance
Lightning Source LLC
Chambersburg PA
CBHW060321220326
41598CB00027B/4390